Strength
Unveiled

by
Margaret L. Deeds

Strength Unveiled
Copyright © 2015 by Margaret Deeds

ISBN: 978-0692390276

Printed in the United States of America

Author's Note

This book is based on the entirety of my mother's life during which she grew stronger and more courageous to fight the difficult trials she faced in the death of loved ones and in facing many other things including divorce and bringing me up, etc.

The rose on the cover of this book represents her - beautiful, slim, bright, and very lovely to look at. You can see that it is strong on the inside and will not easily fall apart. She was like that too. I hope this book can be an inspiration to others as my mother was to me.

Sincerely,
Margaret L. Deeds

Preface

While only a very young girl, Elizabeth lost her mother. The very important thing is that, while at the tender age of nine years, her father and others taught her to look to the Lord Jesus for fortification. When a young child loses a parent, it is extremely important to introduce him or her to the abounding hope which can only be found in a never-ending faith in Jesus, our Lord. All children, of course, will eventually need this; but when a parent dies, this must become a part of their life right away. While a child is very young, he or she is going through a very sensitive and vulnerable time of life. Anything that occurs can have a radical effect which will also impact the rest of his or her life.

From the time she was only nine years of age, she had to learn to be able to take on the responsibilities which her mother would have had. She learned to clean, cook, and sew; and she managed very well. She was prepared for wifely duties at an early age. The important thing is that she also learned to let Jesus' light shine upon her while she was young, and He shone His light upon her throughout her life.

My cry out to the world is: *Don't be defeated today and pass this on to the future of the world. Defeat in life stems from ignorance of God and Jesus*

Christ. With each day, under the counsel of God and Jesus, we can all be winners in life.

Think of Moses when he led the Jews to the Red Sea and God opened the waters so they could cross over to their own homeland. Then, the people were joyous and danced in ludicrous ways and mocked God. Shortly after Moses returned from Mount Sinai with the ten commandments, they began to realize how essential it is to love, honor, and respect God. He is the Alpha and Omega in life.

The main reasons for the degradation of the social realm of man are as follows:

1. Refusal to follow God's Word
2. Refusal to pray and ask forgiveness for one's sins, through Jesus our Savior
3. Excess self pride

When one forgets the Bible and takes not the time nor the thought to ask forgiveness of one's sins, pride and selfishness do filter into one's mind; and one is often so overcome with pride and material gain to the point of being a lost soul. Trials can come upon him, and he immediately becomes even more lost and confused. He is lost in a world without love. In the long run, without the help of God, man has never been able to be truly secure. With faith in Jesus, even as much as a tiny mustard seed, all things are possible. Praise the Lord!

Love Everlasting In Jesus

Thou shalt love the Lord thy God

with all thy heart, and

with all thy soul, and

with all thy strength, and

with all thy mind; and

thy neighbor as thyself.

Luke 10:27

Fly Like A Dove

To all who have become widows, I write this book,
My Mom was a widow and also I, but just take a look.

This life on earth is so very, very short,
But Jesus will give you plenty of support.

My mother learned while she was so young,
How it feels to lose a very dear loved one.

Death often rears its awesome ugly face,
And takes those whom we love without a trace.

Through all of our mourning we must not be
discouraged,
If they are saved by the Lord, all the more to be
encouraged.

Though earthly bodies are dead, the soul lives on
In a much better place, the kingdom of heaven.

We should rejoice at this wonderful feat.
Their hard life on this earth is finally complete.

Dear Lord in heaven, help me not be selfish,
And live in this world and try more to embellish

The love of God and His Word that is so essential,
To ask for His strength which is so very special.

It's for Jesus' sake you should live and He you should love,
Learn from His Word and you will fly through like a dove.

~

Psalms 42:5 ~ *Why art thou cast down, O my soul? and why art thou disquieted in me? hope thou in God: for I shall yet praise him for the help of his countenance.*

Psalm 55:22 ~ *Cast thy burden upon the Lord, and he shall sustain thee: he shall never suffer the righteous to be moved.*

John 16:33 ~ *These things I have spoken unto you, that in me ye might have peace. In the world ye shall have tribulation: but be of good cheer; I have overcome the world.*

Table of Contents

My Mom - An Eternal Rose

As flowing breezes of thought whisk through my troubled brain, precious memories of my Mom usurp my total being. She was such a refined woman who was more than due all the respect and honor which I failed to give her. These words are coming from her daughter who tried, to no avail, to get along with her. In the end, there unfortunately was no way to expunge the bruises of the past. We may have lacked in harmony, but she was always the ultimate of finesse, intelligence, and demureness that I always wished I would someday be able to acquire. Of course, I could never match up to her.

Though beautiful and attractive while she was young and only with a touch of make-up, her beauty increased with each year that she aged. Don't let that fool you though. While being a bleached blond during a time when blondes were associated with being stupid, she was certainly no dimwit. No one could outsmart her, especially me. Many inquired about how far she advanced in college; however, she did not attend. She did, however, graduate from high school with honors.

Her whole life was characterized by diligence in home decor, absolute cleanliness, and all the other important matters of homemaking. While only nine years old, after the loss of her mother, she was taught by her mother's mother about the importance of proprieties in life, good manners, and speaking softly with respect and regard for everyone. Her remarks to me would oftentimes be, "Well, that was very rude," or maybe "That is just not proper and is very disrespectful." Many times I thought of her as "stuck up" with all of her pompous proprieties and such. I was wrong about this. She was teaching me for my own good.

Her skin was without flaw. Her eyes were penetrating with icy blue and green hues. Her hair was brunette, and because of the fairness of her skin, she looked good as a blonde too.

Mom and I were so close after Daddy died when I was only eight years old. She endured so well the loss of her dearly beloved husband. I asked her once if she ever cried, and her reply was, "Oh yes, I just do it when no one is around. There's no need for me to get anyone else upset, though my heart bleeds for him." It was a big transition for her, but she had an enlightened attitude, and I remember her telling me that "all things work together for the best." She would also say, "God knows what's best," and "Don't worry. We'll be all right. Just pray and ask for Jesus to give us His strength, and have faith in Him." She was so reassuring that I really do believe there wasn't anything that my Mom wouldn't be able to handle with ease and resilience, and this proved to be true as the years went on.

Mom, with all of her propriety and good manner, was really a person who appreciated the simple things in life. Oh, how I remember her planting pansies with me when I was about three years old. I can picture it now. We were living in Greenville, South Carolina. There was a low, white, picket fence surrounding the front yard which was filled with rich, green grass. It was spring and the signs of it were beautiful. Mom said, "You must be very gentle while planting pansies, for they are a very sensitive flower." I don't know why this stands out as one of my favorite memories.

Oftentimes she would fry chicken and make potato salad to prepare for us to go to the park and have a picnic with Daddy while he was on lunch break. She cooked so well, and everything was always so scrumptious. She told me that her own grandma and her nanny, Bertha, taught her the art of southern cooking. She said one time, "You know, I used to cook for my own Dad and my brother from the time I was twelve years old."

As I've said, she loved the simple things in life. She always remarked about that refreshing scent of rain that stimulates the senses before it actually falls from the sky above. She also loved roses so much that her favorite perfume was "Joy," which has a luscious rose scent. She loved to feed the blue jays which would fly into the kitchen to land on the stove and wait patiently for her to feed them. She loved having pets too.

Mom loved shopping for clothes and had very good taste in what she would wear. She was also a very careful and frugal shopper. She taught me the importance of getting a good deal on quality merchandise. I remember her words, "Get the feel of the material and make sure that it's not flimsy," and "Check the inside seams for quality sewing and finishing." "Don't buy anything just for the name brand." We had so much fun shopping together. Many times we would just shop and buy nothing. Then she would find a coffee shop and treat us to cheesecake with strawberries and hot chocolate. That was such a treat!

She was born with the name, Elizabeth Edmonia McBride. She was of Irish-English descent. After her first marriage she became Elizabeth McBride Brennan. A name signifies history and descent, and there is no way that I could justifiably write just a few paragraphs to portray the entire background of her names.

Maybe Mom and I had a very hard time getting along with each other while and after I went through my teens, but we shared so much together, through hard times as well as good times. Our life together remains a great and valued relationship which we both shared. She, though passed on now, remains as a sort of icon to me of a truly refined woman and loving mother. There is not a day that I don't think of her.

~

Exodus 20:12 ~ *Honor thy father and thy mother: that the days may be long upon the land which the Lord thy God giveth thee.*

1 John 3:18 ~ *My little children, let us not love in word, neither in tongue; but in deed and in truth.*

Colossians 3:20 ~ *Children, obey your parents in all things: for this is well pleasing to the Lord.*

The Word of God

Many lessons we all must learn.
One thing for sure we must always discern:

The bad way, the good way, the way of the Lord,
All of us surely are caught in this fiord.

Intrepidly on we go forth to battle,
Good knowledge and wisdom will help us to settle.

The Lord's Word of truth enlightens our way,
If only we would study it each and every day.

It's sometimes hard to know our purposes in life,
But Jesus will reveal them; the Word's like a knife.

Hebrews 4:12 ~ *For the word of God is living and powerful, and sharper than any two-edged sword, piercing even to the division of soul and spirit, and of joints and marrow, and is a discerner of the thoughts and intents of the heart.* (NKJ)

Grandma's Soul Has Been Lifted

It was autumn of 1929 in Richmond, Virginia and all the beautiful colors in the trees were cascading along the two-lane road which led to the city. They shone with a glorious array of fuchsia, gold, tan, and brown colors which would normally delight anyone while traveling there. This was a sad day, though. Evan McBride was driving an old model T Ford with his two children inside...Elizabeth, who was nine years of age, and Leonard, who was seven years old. They were going to the funeral of his dearly beloved and now deceased wife, Maime Le'Ann McBride.

Elizabeth Edmonia, my mother, and Leonard Evan, her brother, sat quietly in a state of grief. Liz couldn't take it anymore and finally spoke out in anguish, "Daddy, why did God take Mommy away from us? We need her! Doesn't God know that? It's not fair! I don't understand why God would do this to us! It's just...it's just...it's just MEAN of Him to do this to us! Why is this?! What did we do wrong?"

"Elizabeth, do not be angry with God," her father gently exhorted. "Your mother's heart was not strong, and she had been in anguishing pain for a long time before she died. She just didn't let you know. You probably don't understand now while you are so young, but God actually did her a favor by taking her now so she wouldn't keep on suffering as she was.

"I want her to come back! I miss her!"

"Don't worry, darling. She's probably up with the angels in heaven now. We do still have each other, and now we need to pray to Jesus and ask for His strength to help all of us get through this awful loss. Mommy doesn't want you to be unhappy. It is all right for you to cry now, but as young as you both are, God will help us all get through this."

"That's so easy for you to say, Daddy. I feel like the lining of my heart is broken and emptied out. It hurts so much, Daddy. I feel like...I feel like it's just no use."

"Elizabeth, you must be strong, and I'll say it again: your only strength right now will come from Jesus; and also from all three of us helping one another to stay bonded together. Pray to Jesus, and He will be right there with you to help you along. Just believe in Him. You know this is not easy for me either."

"Yes, but Daddy, you don't seem to be hurting at all!"

"Oh, yes I do hurt terribly. You see, life is not an easy road for us, nor anyone else, to travel through. I'm so sorry that you're having to learn this at such a young age. Another thing is that your whole life is going to be a learning process. You must be sure to read your Bible, keep praying and learning and leaning on the Lord, whether times may be bad or good. This is the only way to find happiness through all the trials and tribulations we face, both in life and in death situations."

"Daddy, what's trials and tribulations?"

"These can often be difficult situations wherein one must make decisions as to how to handle them. These are also times when God may be testing you as to how much true faith you have in Him. You know, because of this, you may be a very strong woman someday. I love you, sweetheart, and I love you, Lenny. Don't let your hearts trouble you. We are going to be all right. As I said, it's all right to go ahead and cry, just don't let your sadness overcome your whole life. We are only in this world for a short time. Someday, when years have passed, we will go to heaven and be with Mommy, but when that time is to be will only be up to God...not you or I."

They arrived finally to the funeral which carried on as scheduled. Maime Le'Ann McBride was laid to rest underneath a very large and full oak tree in October of 1929.

After the funeral, Evan, while he was driving back to Springhill Farm, which was situated in the outskirts of Richmond, Virginia, was a little bit uneasy. Of course, he hid his tears from his children. All of a sudden, he took notice of the grandeur of the autumn foliage along the road traveling homeward and said, "Children, there is still beauty in life. Look at the colors of the leaves out there. Those leaves lived green and vibrant through the spring and summer. Now they have turned many colors to delight us for this season. They will fall, and the trees will produce more leaves next spring. Thank the Lord for this beautiful earth."

As they came closer to the farm, Evan noticed that his sister, Elinore, and her husband, Thomas Jorgansen's car was parked way down the long driveway, close to the house. This was a very gratifying sight to him, and the children were delighted.

Thomas would always bring presents from all over the world or wherever he might have been stationed. He was in the Air Force and traveled to many countries. Very rarely did he and his wife have a chance to visit. This was a wonderful and unexpected surprise.

"Daddy! It's Uncle Tom and Aunt Elee! They're here! They're here!"

Evan's and his children's hearts were filled with excitement. The visit was uplifting after the sadness and solemnity of the funeral. It is so comforting when families come together and love one another and give moral support to each other. God gave us the ability to love, and we should love and cherish our families always.

Psalms 4:1 ~ *Hear me when I call, O God of my righteousness: thou hast enlarged me when I was in distress; have mercy upon me, and hear my prayer.*

Psalms 4:6 ~ *There be many that say, Who will shew us any good? Lord, lift thou up the light of thy countenance upon us.*

Little Children

Little children, be of good cheer,
Your dawn of life has been broken and Jesus is always
here.

Lift up your heads with a bright smile,
For the Lord does love you all the while.

Those wondering eyes of innocent youth
Enlighten my soul to tell you the truth.

Run and play and enjoy this time,
While minding your parents; be good and be fine.

Life is a wonderment during these days,
So much to be learned, it all seems a haze.

But as you grow, you will find
Things could get stormy, but don't you mind.

It's just life's experiences that teach us well
To love and have faith in Jesus, and not to rebel.

If there's ever a time that you feel afraid,
Just pray to Jesus and be not dismayed.

Provoke not your parents who love you so,
For you'll come of age when they must let go.

They're helping and guiding you to fly like a bird,
Listen to their instruction, all important to be heard.

When you grow up it's important to know
God's Word is the truth and through it you must flow.

Many today balk and squirm at even the thought of
God,
But woe to the poor lost souls of ICHABOD.*

Lean not on thine own understanding
And look to God's Word and have faith never ending.

Along the long road of life you will find
Through Jesus you'll have happiness and peace of
mind.

~

*ICHABOD means *without glory to God*

Reference to Ichabod is found in 1 Samuel 4:21:
And she named the child Ichabod, saying, "The glory is departed from Israel" because the ark of God was taken, and because of her father-in-law and her husband.

She was the daughter-in-law of Eli and wife of Phinehas. She was with child and after her travail, named her son "Ichabod" as a result of being on the verge of dying.

~

Matthew 19:13-14 ~ *Then were there brought unto him little children, that He should put His hands on them, and pray: and the disciples rebuked them. But Jesus said, "Suffer little children, and forbid them not, to come unto me: for of such is the kingdom of heaven."*

Cleanse My Soul, Oh My Lord

As Evan was slowly approaching home, while driving down the long driveway, he excitedly blared out of the car window, "Elinore! Tom! I thought you wouldn't be able to come."

He rushed to park the car so he could get out quickly. His heart was pounding with excitement and surprise.

"Elee, were you at the funeral? I didn't see you."

With her warm, loving smile, she attempted to explain, and Thomas immediately took over before she could even utter a sound.

"Evan, I didn't think we'd be able to come, for sure. But I explained to my senior officers that there had been a family tragedy, and I asked, in a pleading way, if they would please allow me time to attend the funeral and try to be of some assistance as it is needed now. Surprisingly, they were more than happy to grant my request."

"But Tom, how did you get here? Where are you based now?"

"Well, it's about an eight or nine hour drive from Charlotte, North Carolina, where I am based right now. Listen, I know how close you and your sister, Elinore, are and this is one time that you really need for her to be with you and help you get back on your feet. So I'll stay for a few days and leave Elee here for a couple of weeks and come back to pick her up."

Regardless, Elinore was aware that Tom had only a few days leave, and she wanted to get started as soon as possible so Tom wouldn't have to drive all that way back for her. She checked the classified ads of the newspaper and went on to set up interviews for a number of women who desired to be a full-time nanny. The actual job would consist of being a nanny to two children, a housekeeper, a laundress, and a cook. It certainly wasn't easy to find someone who would do all of this, but with her determination, she would find the right person. Having a knack for good judgment of character, she was fortunate enough to meet someone suitable and trustworthy right away. She chose a middle-aged woman name Bertha Simms to live at the Springhill home and accomplish all of these tasks. Bertha understood that she was to remain there just for three years, and all the while, she would be teaching Elizabeth everything about home care and economics, to prepare her to take over when she turned twelve years of age.

There she was, Elizabeth Edmonia, at only the age of nine, and so much to be learned in only three years. During those three years, such a feeling of attachment grew between both Elizabeth and Bertha.

It was February of 1931 and Elizabeth was nearing her eleventh birthday, which would be on the 15th of March. It was so very cold and dreary a day even though the sun would slightly peek through the dark clouds every now and then. Liz dragged herself steadily through the slowly melting snow and stumbled up the front porch steps after her ten mile walk from school on this Friday afternoon. She was relieved that it was finally the end of the week. Upon opening the door, there came Bertha.

"Hurry child! Get in here and take off your boots and wet clothes. It's so cold and that slush is terrible outside. I don't want you to walk it all over the house that I worked all day to clean!"

"Oh Bertha, I'm so very tired, and I feel all worn out."

"It's all right, Liz. Just do as I say and then take yourself in to take a nice, hot bath. That will make you feel better."

She listlessly took Bertha's advice, and after dinner, Liz curiously wandered over to Bertha's room. At her young age, she did ponder about all of this fuss about keeping the house so clean and taking so many baths and always washing her hands.

"Bertha," she lightly called so as not to greatly disturb her. "Bertha, are you there? Are you dressed? I need to talk with you please!"

"Come in, Sweetheart." There she sat, comfortably dressed for bed and relaxing to read a book after having worked so hard all day. "Tell me. What could be troubling your mind at this time dear girl?"

"Berti, I'm just confused about why or what the reason is for working so hard to clean house all day and having to take a bath so often, and always washing my hands even though they're not dirty."

"Elizabeth, you are so young that you don't realize that if you don't keep squeaky clean, you could catch a disease or get sick from little tiny germs which you can't see with your eyes. Germs live and multiply in filth."

Bertha could see the look of wonderment that fell upon the face of youth unaware. "Yes, Elizabeth, you could get very sick if you don't keep yourself clean."

"Well, I guess I understand now. Thank you Bertha." She started to walk out of Bertha's room.

"Wait! Elizabeth, come back here. There is something that is most important for you to know. Sit down and listen very carefully. Though you may not understand this now, you need to learn this also. In the Bible, God teaches us that we are to keep ourselves clean. Now, did you know that?"

"No, Berti. Why is this," she asked inquisitively?

"Did you know that your body is the temple of God's Holy Spirit?"

"Is this true? You mean... Oh!"

Gently, Bertha replied, "Yes, dear. Your body is not yours alone to do with as you wish. The Holy Spirit of God lives within you. I'll teach you more about this when you get a little older."

"No! Please! I want for you to tell me about this now!"

"All right child. It's never too early for you to learn the teachings of the Bible and what God commands us all to do in our lives."

Bertha read and explained the following verses straight from the Scriptures written in the bible:

1 Corinthians 6:19-20 ~ *What? know ye not that your body is the temple of the Holy Ghost which is in you, which ye have of God, and ye are not your own? For ye are bought with a price: therefore glorify God in your body, and in your spirit, which are God's.*

Isaiah 52:11 ~ *Depart ye, depart ye, go ye out from thence, touch no unclean thing; go ye out of the midst of her (Zion); be ye clean, that bear the vessels of the Lord.*

Luke 11:39 ~ *And the Lord said unto him, "Now do ye Pharisees make clean the outside of the cup and the platter; but your inward part is full of ravening and wickedness."*

Bertha was a truly wonderful person. She taught Elizabeth what she should remember about house cleaning and cleanliness. To top it off, she understood and explained the precepts of God. She made a very good impression on both children.

In October of 1932, Elizabeth was well prepared to take on the responsibilities approaching her for then and for the future.

It was October and beautiful leaves were slowly falling from the trees as hearts were trying not to break. To both of the children, it was so hard to see Bertha leave the household; she had become like a second mother to Elizabeth and Leonard but she could not stay with them any longer. I can only imagine the empty-heart feeling and the lump in her throat that Elizabeth felt as she had to say her last goodbye to Bertha Simms.

Proverbs 22:6 ~ *Train up a child in the way he should go: and when he is old, he will not depart from it.*

Cleanse My Soul, Oh My Lord

Oh how the wind whistles through the chimes of time.
I have not yet heard a sound so sublime.

Through the path of life we all must go,
And remember always that Jesus loves us so.

Though dirt and filth engulf this earth,
We must always cleans our bodies, souls, and girth.

It's not hard to adapt to outward cleanliness,
But we know that being clean is next to godliness.

There's just one thing I forgot to mention:
We must cleanse our souls to find redemption.

Only God knows the thoughts and intentions of our
hearts and minds,
We must clean up our sinful thoughts and endeavor to
be kind.

Cleanse my soul, Oh my Lord, I do cry
To lift up my thoughts and intents before I die.

Lead me not to just cleanse the outside of my cup,
But to try to think like the Lord Jesus and clean my
thoughts up.

No one on earth can be perfectly clean,
Just read the Lord's Word and you'll know what I mean.

Bless the Lord, Oh my soul, and all that is within me.
Cleanse my heart and soul so that I may shine into eternity.

Psalms 103:1-4 ~ *Bless the Lord, O my soul: and all that is within me, bless his holy name. Bless the Lord, O my soul, and forget not all his benefits: Who forgiveth all thine iniquities; who healeth all thy diseases; Who redeemeth thy life from destruction; who crowneth thee with lovingkindness and tender mercies.*

Salvation Makes Life Worth Living

Elizabeth found salvation through the blessing of her grandma's guidance, but I don't know her personal testimony, so here is mine:

It was the middle of May 1973 when my husband, Bob, and I moved into a duplex in North Hollywood. We were told about this cute place by some friends, and your eyes would pop out at the meager price of the rent we were asked to pay. The Lord did bless us.

We looked around for a church and happened to go by Calvary Baptist Church. After we went there for a couple of times, Pastor Ashley and George Glover came to visit us one evening. Being that Bob was already a saved Christian, and I wasn't, the conversation was centered on me and my beliefs. Oh how I was on the defensive. The pastor's calmness kept on, but still I wouldn't move my thoughts one bit.

Well, it was the fourth time we had gone to church, and I felt the Lord calling me to walk up that aisle of the church and pray for my salvation. So I went. A good woman and I held a session of prayer to the Lord, asking Him into my heart; and to this day, "He walks with me and He talks with me."

I didn't, then, think baptism was necessary, but I certainly wasn't against it. I later learned that water baptism is the sign of the seal of salvation. The baptism of Jesus on any one person is the death of Jesus on the cross, and the resurrection to life in the Father, the Son, and the Holy Spirit. For everyone to be saved, they go through salvation, which is the baptism of Jesus on the cross and the resurrection.

I then came to find out that after being saved, one must carry the Word to others so that they, also, may be saved unto the salvation of the Lord. It was so wonderful to be able to give over all my guilt for the many sins I had committed to the Lord Jesus so that He would bear them for me. I felt as if I was likened to a wee baby, and at times I was somewhat frightened about the task set before me. However, I was nurtured well in learning to pray, read the Bible and to witness to others to come and share the glory of God.

How very important the Word of God is in our calling to bring others to truly know the Lord.

Here's the Parable of the Sower found in Matthew 13:20-23:

But he that received the seed into stony places, the same is he that heareth the word, and anon with joy receiveth it; yet hath he not root in himself, but dureth for a while: for when tribulation or persecution ariseth because of the word, by and by he is offended. He also that received seed among the thorns is he that heareth the word; and the care of this world, and the deceitfulness of riches, choke the word, and he becometh unfruitful. But he that received seed into the good ground is he that heareth the word, and understandeth it; which also beareth fruit, and bringeth forth, some an hundredfold, some sixty, some thirty.

Be a Woman of Modesty and Silence

Among the commandments written in God's Word,
A woman is to be seen and never to be heard.

It's not so impossible you see,
Man is supposed to be in authority.

A woman must certainly learn respect and good manners,
Modesty, sobriety, and to honor her elders.

In recent years I've often heard, in women
Domineering qualities have increasingly occurred.

There's a thing called women's liberation.
It's a part of society that's been usurping our nation.

Oh, I understand it's because of the national economy,
A mom must work now instead of being a mommy.

Still, we women must effectively learn,
To quiet our mouths and meekly learn.

Respect and modesty are so very important,
Or the feminine gender will slowly become vacant.

The manner in which a woman walks and talks definitely shows
Whether she was taught in her youth and practices as she grows.

God gave us statutes with which we must comply,
Which, regardless of today's society, we must never deny.

Oh yes, for you Lord I constantly seek
To love and obey, to render to be meek.

Please help us to honor your statutes and femininity,
And thus show you our love through all of eternity.

Amen

Galatians 5:22-23 ~ *But the fruit of the Spirit is love, joy, peace, longsuffering, gentleness, goodness, faith, meekness, temperance: against such there is no law.*

1 Peter 3:4 ~ *But let it be the hidden man of the heart, in that which is not corruptible, even the ornament of a meek and quiet spirit, which is in the sight of God of great price.*

Life is a Learning Process

One summer Sunday, while Elizabeth was approximately thirteen years old, she was sitting in the pew of the church after hearing a sermon on prayer. Her inquisitive thoughts got the best of her. She wandered up to the front of the church to see if the preacher would dare take the time to talk to her.

"Pastor Weiss, I need to ask you something important to me. Is it all right for me to pray to the Lord as if I'm talking to Him, or should I just say the Lord's Prayer?"

"Yes, dear, it is all right for you to pray as if you're talking to the Lord; just use the utmost respect and honor towards God, for He is the reason you live. It's a good idea to say the Lord's Prayer also. Did you know that this prayer is found in the Bible under Matthew 6:8-13? You see, the disciples were asking Jesus the same kind of question, and He taught them this prayer so that they would know. However, He also let them know that they must not use vain repetitions."

"What do you mean by vain repetitions?"

"I'll tell you. You see, you don't have to repeat things over and over for the Lord to hear you. You need to pray of course, but the Lord our Father knows what things you have need of before you ask Him. Just to repeat a memorized prayer is not enough. You must honor Him with glory to His holy name, thank Him for His many blessings, and not just pray for yourself, but also you must pray for others. You must also pray in a private place."

"Yes, but we all pray together in church!"

"That's because we go to church to give glory to the Father in fellowship with others who know and love God. We pray together in the house of the Lord. We do this on Sunday which is now our day of rest, but it was God's day of rest after six days of creation."

"Wouldn't it be all right for me to pray anywhere?"

"It's all right child. Just don't make a public show of it. You can be anywhere and just pray within yourself, but it's best to also pray on a regular basis in a private place."

Innocently, Liz looked to the Pastor and said, "What should I do to learn more?"

"Elizabeth, you must start reading the Bible, and learning what the Lord wants for you to do in life. Here, I'll read you some verses that might help you:

Philippians 4:4-7 ~ *Rejoice in the Lord always: and again I say rejoice. Let your moderation be known unto all men. The Lord is at hand. Be careful for nothing; but in every thing by prayer and supplication with thanksgiving, let your requests be known unto God. And the peace of God, which passeth all understanding, shall keep your hearts and minds through Christ Jesus. "*

"Thank you, Pastor Weiss. I can tell that I really have a lot to study and to learn."

"That's what life is all about, dear. Life is a learning process, and you can always learn just by the scriptures of the Bible."

Oh, the influence this had on Elizabeth! She went out of the church on this brightly sunlit day and felt peace in her heart that God was with her always, and she scampered up the streets of Richmond to go and visit Grandma Margaret.

"What's with you child? You look as if you're floating on a white cloud," was Margaret's response upon seeing Liz.

"Grandma, I think Jesus loves me."

"Of course, darling. Jesus loves you and all of His children. God knows all, and He watches over us all the time."

"I asked Pastor Weiss about his sermon on prayer, and all of my answers were right in the Bible."

"That's right dear. The most important book in the world for you to read is God's Word, the Bible. And when you pray, no matter what, He will hear you and love you. You can know that."

Though Liz was a very busy girl and hardly had time to do all that she had to do plus her school work, she would take time to sit down and read a portion of the Bible whenever she could, even if it was only a few verses at a time.

Every Day, a New Day is Born

We awake to the sounds vitalizing each day,
Often inglorious to God; what can I say?

I would get up and dressed and ready for work,
Not even a trite prayer, and this did I shirk.

Until one day, during my years of grieving,
I looked and saw birds and butterflies a winging.

And for all the six days of His grandeur creations,
I felt amiss, ignoring the beauty of God's
manifestations.

And then suddenly one day it came to my mind:
He gave us life eternal, and that's not hard to find.

Just read the Lord's Word diligently,
It's written right there in John, chapter three.

A perfect Christian, no not am I,
My sins are so numerous, so much I could cry.

We've been so endowed by Jesus' horrible death.
God will now forgive, we must repent to escape God's
wrath.

Oh, for more time and prayers should I give,
For Jesus does love us, and yes, He still lives.

So Close But So Distant

Grandma Margaret was a wonderful and very important influence on Elizabeth. It was another beautiful day, during the spring of 1935. Liz had just turned 15 years old, and was on her way to see her Grandma. Flowers were blooming, the grass was a rich green, and the trees looked so full of vitality. Elizabeth was somewhat bothered about an unpleasant occurrence that came between her and her best friend. She sat down on the couch inside her Grandma's house looking so distressed.

"What's wrong Liz? You look so sad and bereaved."

"Grandma, I... Oh! My best friend and I are no longer friends. It just distresses me so that I want to cry my eyes out."

"Liz, what could this have been about? A boyfriend?"

"No, Grandma. She and I were just talking about the Bible and she said that the Bible is untrue, and that there is no God. We argued, and now she wants nothing to do with me anymore."

"Elizabeth, this is a very common reaction that unbelievers have towards Christians. It's very hard, I know, but that's the way it is and has been since the ancient times of the world. You must try to understand, have patience, and be nurturing towards her. She'll come around."

"I don't understand, Grandma. Why is she treating me so badly?"

"Elizabeth, it has been and is because many believe in God but not in Jesus, many believe in other gods, and many don't believe in any gods, just themselves. You see the Bible Scriptures were written by God and His apostles, and it holds the whole truth.

2 Timothy 3:16 says: *All scripture is given by inspiration of God, and is profitable for doctrine, for reproof, for correction, for instruction in righteousness.*

You see, Liz, many won't accept this. They don't want instructions to follow. Also, they don't want to feel that they have to answer to God or anyone about anything. Here's what it says in the Bible about this:

Proverbs 15:10 ~ *Correction is grievous unto him that forsaketh the way: and he that hateth reproof shall die.*

Proverbs 15:14 ~ *The heart of him that hath understanding seeketh knowledge: but the mouth of fools feedeth on foolishness.*

Elizabeth, she probably doesn't hate you, but she just doesn't seem to want to accept the Bible or God. You must pray for her and maybe someday, she will. In the meantime, you can still be her friend, but you may have to find someone else for a best friend. Take this advice from the bible:

2 Thessalonians 3:13-15 ~ *But ye, brethren, be not weary in well doing. And if any man obey not our word by this epistle, note that man, and have no company with him, that he may be ashamed. Yet count him not as an enemy, but admonish him as a brother.*

Mark 13:13 ~ *And ye shall be hated of all men for my name's sake: but he that shall endure unto the end, the same shall be saved.*

Mark 12:30 ~ *And thou shalt love the Lord thy God with all thy heart, and with all thy soul, and with all thy mind, and with all thy strength: this is the first commandment.*

Try to memorize this last passage about loving the Lord and obeying his Word, Liz"

"It's so very hard, Grandma. We've been such good friends for about three years now. I love her as a dear friend, and...well, it just hurts me so much."

"Elizabeth, you are going to learn that people do change as they grow older, especially during their teen years. However, it is very important for you to learn to be patient, have understanding, and always have a forgiving heart. This disagreement does not have to make you two harshly against each other. You just probably won't be as close as you once were. Pray for her soul, and love her in this way:

36

Luke 6:37 ~ *Judge not, and ye shall not be judged: condemn not, and ye shall not be condemned: forgive, and ye shall be forgiven."*

"Thank you, Grandma. I think everything may somehow work out. Maybe time will take care of it. I really need to study the Bible more. It seems to have all the answers for life's predicaments."

Love and Forgiveness are Essential

A good friendship, gone bad, hurts my whole being,
Impediments on my heart snare me from fleeing.

I look and wonder: what did I do
To cause such an upset, and it breaks my heart too.

She was so joyous and fun to be with,
But now, joy is gone. It's just like a myth.

To understand life and all it's probabilities,
At youth will I learn to adapt to new facilities.

I know not what is deep in the soul
Of each new friend, for God is in control.

Patience, understanding and forgiveness I must have,
For who am I to judge, with the sinful soul I have?

Lean not to thine own understanding,
But trust in the Lord is God's commanding.

Trust and obey, and love will abound,
It rings in my ears, and I like that sound.

I forgive my friend, for she meant no ill,
I'll pray for her soul and support her still.

Thank you, Lord, for easing my mind,
Always you're with me and ever so kind.

AMEN

Sweet Sixteen

It was a chilly morning in March of 1936, just before the breaking of dawn. The thin, ruffled curtains jostled about with a cool breeze, whispering through the window by Elizabeth's bed.

With a sudden awakening, Liz jumped out of bed, realizing that she forgot to set her alarm clock the night before. It was a matter of habit that she luckily awakened early, and she was relieved that she hadn't slept later than she did. She scurried to get ready for the day. After showering and dressing, she ran out to milk the cow, then made breakfast, and finally sat down to eat with her father and her brother. Her birthday was coming up in just three days, and she was going to turn sixteen years of age.

Her father spoke, "Why are you looking so bright and peppy on this morning?"

"Daddy, don't you know? I'm going to be sixteen years old coming this Saturday! They say that a girl begins to enter the stage of womanhood at this age."

"Of course! I do realize that and I'm very happy for you. I can see a very bold twinkling in your eyes. There's something more on your mind than that though. I can tell. What is it?"

Shyly, she looked at him. "Uh, Bo Scarborough asked me if I'd like to go out for dinner on a date with him...to celebrate my birthday. May I go Daddy? Please!"

"Well, this would be your first date, honey. I don't know. Tell me about this young man. How old is he? Also, how did you come to meet him? I would want to meet him before you go out on a date together."

"Daddy, he is seventeen, and I met him during lunchtime last week. He is a very nice person. I think you will like him. He is one of the best players on the football team. I know that I do have a crush on him. Practically all the girls at school want to go out with him."

"Oh. Great! Let me tell you something, young lady. You must be careful! Just because a young man is considered very handsome and is on the football team doesn't mean that he is necessarily a good person or that he has good intentions. The fact is that he's the type of person that you'd better watch out for."

"But Dad, he is a good person. He gets good grades in school. And he also says that he love me!"

"Wait a minute! Just how long did you say that you've actually known him?

"I met him at lunchtime while we were waiting in line last week, and we've been having lunch together every day since them."

41

"Now look, Liz. You're probably going through a phase of 'puppy love' right now. True love doesn't start as only a matter of love at first sight. There's much more to love than that. It takes time and getting to know each other in a far different way than just attraction to one another. He doesn't even know that he loves you. I just want you to be careful and not let him turn you around and break your heart. One thing is very important for you to remember all the time you are with him. Whatever you do, hold onto your virginity and do not have sexual intercourse together. If you promise me that, then I'll let you go out together."

"Thank you Daddy!" I promise I won't have sex with anyone until after I have been married to him."

1 Thessalonians 4:3 ~ *For this is the will of God, even your sanctification, that ye should abstain from fornication.*

1 John 2:16-17 ~ *For all that is in the world, the lust of the flesh, and the lust of the eyes, and the pride of life, is not of the Father, but is of the world. And the world passeth away, and the lust thereof: but he that doeth the will of God abideth for ever.*

"I tell you what, Liz. We'll celebrate your birthday on Sunday afternoon and we'll all go out to dinner then too. Just make sure that I have a chance to meet Bo on Saturday, before you two go out. I would like to speak to him. That would be proper."

As it went, Elizabeth went out with Bo on Saturday and they enjoyed a wonderful meal together at the Colfax Restaurant, which was considered to be the nicest one in Richmond at that time. Everything was very happy and enjoyable. Of course, Bo knew that he'd better be careful and not make any attempts that he might end up regretting.

During the next week of school, Liz happened to be talking to her friends and she heard that there were rumors going around that Bo and Linda Clausen, who was also a senior, had been going steady with each other since way before Liz met him. He had given her his class ring to wear just a week after his date with Liz.

The sudden knowledge of this set Elizabeth's heart on fire. Right away, she went to Linda Clausen and asked if she was going steady with Bo. Of course, she didn't know Linda, so she didn't want to mention anything about her date with Bo. She just went on about her business.

With a big lump in her throat, Elizabeth trudged herself home from school, trying to hold back her tears. She got home, and after preparing dinner, she waited for her father to come home from work. When Evan walked inside, Liz ran to him, putting her arms around him and hugging him.

"What's this? Are you all right? You look as if you've been crying!"

"Oh Daddy, I now know you were right about Bo. He didn't really love me! Tell me why people say things when they don't really mean them."

"You will learn, dear. Both of you are young, and at your age, you're just beginning to learn about love and this world we live in. You must remember not to rush yourself to fall in love. When you do meet the right young man, you will know it, but you must give yourselves at least a few months to learn about how much you have in common with each other, before you can really say that you love him. You should learn from this experience."

"Yes, thank you, Dad. I love you."

After this occurrence, Elizabeth dated other young men, but her heart remained with Bo, even though they never had anything to do with each other again. In a way, he was her very first heart throb and her first love. That was hard to let go.

Jude 1:7 ~ *Even as Sodom and Gomorrha, and the cities about them in like manner, giving themselves over to fornication, and going after strange flesh, are set forth as an example...*

1 Corinthians 6:9 ~ *Know ye not that the unrighteous shall not inherit the kingdom of God? Be not deceived: neither fornicators, nor idolaters, nor adulterers, nor effeminate, nor abusers of themselves with mankind...*

Loving Advice

The wonder of love and all it can be,
While young, we reach out for it impetuously.

Children are influenced by adults every day,
Infuse the love of God, and lead them His way.

All the days of a child's growing up years,
You're obligated to teach and advise them, instead of
their peers.

Infiltrate their hearts with love always abounding,
Read to them Psalms of David which are ever
reminding:

Precious is the heart that loves God with all soul and
mind,
Later on, teach them about love of a different kind.

Impart to them truly a very specific fact:
That love requires devotion and is not just a pact.

Young love can become aglow just in one day.
Tell them to be sure that it's not just an attractive
array.

The world is abounding with love and hate,
Youth are unsure as they seek the right trait.

Their hormones consume them to turn to lust,
Confusion sets in, and they think that they must.

Their bodies are infused in the search for love,
While God gave his commandment from above:

Thou shalt not commit fornication,
And this He did order, with love for His creation.

Sexual relations should be only part of marriage,
With intentions to unite and help form a new age.

Regenerate young lives with inspirational verses,
Trust in the Lord, and there will be no remorses.

John 15:10 ~ *If ye keep my commandments, ye shall abide in my love; even as I have kept my Father's commandments, and abide in His love.*

Psalms 143:8 ~ *Cause me to hear thy lovingkindness in the morning; for in thee do I trust...*

Departing to a New Home

It was December of 1938 and Elizabeth was now almost 19 years old. She had graduated from high school with honors in June of 1938. Evan did not have the intention of sending her to college, as he did not feel the need to. She was a great part of the home. He often did ponder about her getting married someday, but he just left that in God's hands.

On one cold and frosty Friday, he realized how overly tired he had become after a very hardworking week. So many people seemed to need him this week and he felt frazzled. His office was full of patients, all day, every day. He had a good reputation as being a good dentist and was glad to have the trust of so many people.

At 5:30pm that day, his receptionist called out to Evan "Dr. McBride, you have a long distance call from Birmingham, Alabama. Are you busy right now?"

Immediately, he thought it might be an emergency call from his sister, Elinore. His automatic reply was, "No, I'm not busy. I'll be right there!"

Picking up the phone, he said, "Yes? This is Dr. McBride."

"Evan, this is Elinore. Sorry to call you at work, but I just must speak to you now. Don't worry.

It's not an emergency. I figured that you'd be getting ready to go home about now anyway."

"That's fine. It's good to hear from you. What's on your mind? Is everything all right?"

"Oh yes, we are both healthy and doing very well. Tom has been given the rank of Lt. Colonel. Just after his promotion, he was offered to be transferred to March Air Force Base in Riverside, California. We'll be leaving in January and we want to come and visit you before we travel so far away from you. If you haven't got any other plans for Christmas, could we come and celebrate it with you and the children?"

"Yes, of course! That would be great! I'll look forward to seeing you both."

"Evan, I have a Springfield cured and smoked ham, and I'll be sure to help prepare it and all the trimmings, so tell Liz not to worry. She need not cook anything. It would be a nice time for my daughters, Victoria and Anne, to spend some time together with Liz and Len. They needn't be distant cousins forever."

"Oh, Elee, Leonard is married now to a fine young girl. Her name is Jenny and they live in the city of Richmond, but they will both be here. I'll make sure of that. Elizabeth is still here at Springhill, and I know that she'll be so elated that you are coming this Christmas. Thank you, dear, for this wonderful news. Now, although I am tired, I feel uplifted and happy."

Yes, it was a wonderful Christmas, indeed. During this time, Elizabeth finally had the opportunity to get to know her cousins, and they enjoyed being together. It was such a warm and homey feeling in the house with so many relatives that were able to get together at such a joyous time of the year.

It was the day after Christmas when Elinore approached Evan about Elizabeth. "Evan, I am concerned about Liz. Is she in love with or dating anyone, or is she going to go to college? Just what is she planning to with her life?"

"No, she is not dating nor in love with anyone. And I don't believe that I have enough money to send her to college. She does still go to her Grandma's house quite often for tea."

"Evan, she needs to spread her wings and fly. Now, don't be upset with me, please. We are talking about Elizabeth and what might be good for her. Would you be willing to let Liz come back with us to California? She and her cousins get along so well. I think it would be good for her to have a mother figure like myself in her life."

"Elinore! I'll be all alone then."

"Now Evan. You're going to have to let go soon, or else your own selfishness will keep Liz from having a life of her own."

"You are right. Thank you Elinore. I guess it would be a good idea for her to go with you and Tom. I know that I can trust you to take good care of her. She isn't going to meet anyone by just staying on this farm all the time."

At dinner that evening, after everyone prayed grace, Elinore popped the big question to Liz in front of everyone. "Elizabeth, you're 18 now, and since you're not going to be able to go to college, would you like to go with us to California to live for a little while?"

"Oh yes! But what about Daddy?"

"I'll be all right, Honey. You need to get away from this farm and go someplace where you can have more of an opportunity to have some fun with your cousins and maybe even, someday, meet a fine young gentleman and get married."

Liz was so excited that she started packing that night. Her father came in and said, "Elizabeth, I want you to know that I'm not just trying to get rid of you. I will miss you deeply. I just want to leave you with a few verses from the Bible that are meaningful to me at this time:

Ruth 3:10, 11 ~ *And Boaz said, Blessed be thou of the Lord, my daughter: for thou has shewed more kindness in the latter end than at the beginning, inasmuch as thou followedst not young men, whether poor or rich. And now, my daughter, fear not; I will do to thee all that thou requirest: for all the city of my people doth know that thou art a virtuous woman.*

2 Timothy 3:15 ~ *...and that from a child thou hast known the holy scriptures, which are able to make thee wise unto salvation through faith which is in Christ Jesus."*

"Thank you Daddy. I know that you tell me those verses with all your heart. I love you so very much, and I will miss you!"

She left with the Jorgansens a few days later to go and live with them on March Air Force Base, about 25 miles outside Riverside, California. This was definitely a big change for the course of Elizabeth's life. A good one. Every daughter needs a mother, and this was so good for her.

Impart the Love of Jesus

Many children are born each and every day,
It's not God's will that they be led astray.

How difficult it can be to be the only parent,
We must try, though, to make it evident.

Jesus, who lived and suffered the cross did not depart,
A renewed life begins when we accept Him into our heart.

A father's love for his daughter is totally true,
When he realizes she needs very much a mother, too.

It's easy for me to say this in black and white,
Finding a new mate can be a somewhat desperate plight.

Important it is to be family oriented right now,
Often, relatives can assist, if indeed you allow.

A boy needs a father to instruct in his way,
A girl needs a mother to guide her in her way.

In any case, it's most imperatively known,
A child instilled with the Word of Jesus will be victoriously grown.

Be still and remember, a child's adult life is at hand,
Pray, read the Gospel, and God will give you a hand.

Psalms 120:1 ~ *In my distress I cried unto the Lord, and he heard me.*

Psalms 124:8 ~ *Our help is in the name of the Lord, who made heaven and earth.*

Ephesians 6:4 ~ *And, ye fathers, provoke not your children to wrath: but bring them up in the nurture and admonition of the Lord.*

A Rose in Bloom

Elizabeth's life was like a flower bud finally in the process of blooming. Her cousins were like sisters to her, and they shared much together. Aunt Elinore was very strict, but she loved them all, each in her own way to make sure they were brought up well. She, very adequately, made a good impression on them to mind whatever she told them. She was also very open to discuss with each girl privately any problems or quandaries that she might have.

It was 1940 and World War II was on. At the time, the Germans, after having won a quiet victory in the country of Poland, were going on to occupy Norway and Denmark. The reason Hitler was insistent about Norway was because he wanted to seize the thick-water plant which was there. This was what was used to make the atomic bomb. Due to known leaks of this information, the plant was destroyed before Hitler got his grip on it.

During this time, so much was going on with all the U. S. armed forces. The air force was really the Army Air Corps., and Colonel Jorgansen had a lot to accomplish while preparing the young lieutenants for their service in the war.

While discussing an important mission with some of his top men, it so happened that Lt. Brennan had some intriguing ideas about accomplishing this mission.   Col. Jorgansen wanted to consider these ideas and talk more extensively and privately in his own home.

"Lieutenant Brennan, would you be a guest at my house tonight and have dinner with my family?"

"Yes Sir, Colonel Jorgansen, I'd certainly be honored."

"Be there by 5:30. That will give us an hour to talk in the library before dinner at 6:30."

"Thank you Sir, I'll bring all of my information with me."

"By the way, Lieutenant, tell me about your own personal background.   I'd like to know more about you."

"Sir, my father is a professor of Physiology at the College of William and Mary in Virginia. I was born on October 23, 1917, in Peoria, Illinois. I have a master's degree in Physiology. I entered the U. S. Army Air Corps training center and received my diploma for military aviation in June of last year. Then, I was transferred to March Air Force Base to start my service in the forces."

"Well, Lt. Brennan, I'll look forward to your coming tonight."

It was a cold wet night in December of 1940 when Lt. Brennan came over for dinner. He and the Colonel immediately went into the library for discussion.   Little did the young man know that he would meet and fall in love with the niece of Colonel Jorgansen that very night at the dinner table.

Elizabeth was still shy and a bit quiet. When she met Edward, she even blushed. Ed couldn't take his eyes off of her. He thought, "Can this be my new found love?" Her feminine, coquettish manner attracted him. Though the bitter raindrops had chilled him while he was walking up to the house earlier in the evening, the moment his eyes met hers love was in the air with a good feeling of warmth. After dinner they talked and found that they had a lot in common when they talked about religion.

Being a regular officer in the Air Force often requires that a man in the service spend quite a bit of time going out on different missions when he is appointed to. Sometimes a mission would take up to a week to complete. Regardless of this, any time he had free, he would make sure to spend it with Elizabeth. Their friendship and love grew for a good four months.

In the middle of April, he was given orders to be transferred to an Air Force base near San Francisco by the beginning of June 1941. He decided right away that he was going to marry Liz.

The very next day, with hope in his heart, he approached Col. Jorgansen at noon.

"Col. Jorgansen, sir, I'd like to ask you if you would honor my proposal of marriage to your niece, Elizabeth?"

"Wait a minute! You are a fine young lad and a good officer with promise, but while I would be one to so honor that, I must confer with her father. I'll need for you to be here tomorrow afternoon at 5pm. Then, we will go to my home and I will call her father and speak to him about this. Then you can have dinner with us. Let's just do that. Then, we will see what he has to say, and maybe you will be able to ask him for her hand in marriage. Don't feel that you need to do that right in front of us all, unless you want to."

"Thank you, sir. You've made my day brighter."

"Hold on, Lieutenant. You still need to get her father's permission, but I will help you all I can."

On May 10, 1941, they got married. It was a small but very appropriate wedding with a reception which was held at the Jorgansen's home. Elizabeth's father and brother were both able to come all the way from their homes in Virginia to meet Edward and attend the ceremony and celebrate. Such great happiness was all around.

Isaiah 62:5 ~ *For as a young man marrieth a virgin, so shall thy sons marry thee: and as the bridegroom rejoiceth over the bride, so shall thy God rejoice over thee.*

Isaiah 61:10 ~ *I will greatly rejoice in the Lord, my soul shall be joyful in my God; for he hath clothed me with the garments of salvation, he hath covered me with the robe of righteousness, as a bridegroom decketh himself with ornaments, and as a bride adorneth herself with her jewels.*

Marriage
A Promise To God

Intrinsic in a marriage of a wholesome kind
Is the bride and groom embraced with close friendship
in mind.

Some may think my opinion is ridiculous,
I believe certainly marriage should not be frivolous.

Evidently so, I have seen a great loss of character,
The minds of many blinded, then divorced thereafter.

When a bride and groom make their vows,
Both should realize that they're vowing to God now.

These vows are a promise to God which should not be
broken,
Remember your words; for they're not just a small
token.

Patience, communication, understanding, we certainly
know,
Will vitalize your marriage, helping your strong union
to grow.

In order to have these, an altruistic love of God will help,
To make one not so conscious of one's own self.

Self-pride is the enemy throughout our lives,
It makes one grow weak and weary as the end arrives.

Thrust forth your heart, unselfishly so,
And happy you'll both be and forever aglow.

A Family on the Horizon

By June of 1941, Edward and Elizabeth Brennan had moved from Riverside, California to one of the suburbs in the city of San Francisco, not far from the army air base where he was stationed.

I can see it now...those beautiful rolling hills which, when one gets to the top, he or she can survey the busy city with those red cable cars running up and down the middle of the city streets. Of course, the grandeur of the Golden Gate Bridge can be very interesting if you take the time to find out all that went into the building of it from 1933 to 1937. It has a main span of 4200 feet. Imagine that!

Both Liz and Ed were very eager about starting a family as soon as possible. It wasn't until November of 1941 that Elizabeth had an inkling that she might be pregnant. She went to the doctor and, having confirmed that she was with child, waited eagerly for Edward to come home that night.

"Hello, darling! I'm home!"

"Ed! Oh, honey! I'm so glad you're home!"

"Liz, what's going on? You look like a bubble that's right on the verge of bursting open!"

"Guess what? The doctor gave me the results of my pregnancy test, and..."

"We're going to have a baby?"

"Yes! Yes! Yes!"

"Elizabeth, that's wonderful! We're finally going to have a family. You better be careful, dear. As badly as I want us to start a family, I don't want anything to happen to you. When will the baby be due?"

"I am supposed to have the baby sometime in the middle of next June. It is so great to finally be with child, but I do admit to being a little bit scared. I've heard so much about the pain that comes with the delivery process. Ah well. While it is kind of frightening, I know that it will surely be worth it to us both. I love you honey, and I am so happy! We ought to let your Mom know."

"Yes! We should call her as soon as possible. But don't worry, Liz. You are strong and the doctors will be able to give you something for the pain. Maybe you should have a little talk with my mother about this."

"I am not that worried, I am sure that she had it a lot harder than I'll ever have it. I can't wait to start preparing for our child. Thank you, Edward, I love you so much!"

"I love you too, Liz, and I am looking forward to being a father of many children I hope."

As her pregnancy went on, Liz spoke to some of her other friends who did help ease her mind about the delivery of her new baby. One time, she was thinking and giggling to herself about her wedding night. Ed had said that he wanted her to have just enough babies to form a baseball team. Although he was just joking, she remembered how she promptly sat straight up in bed and said, "Wait a minute! Hold on. You are not going to do that to me!"

On June 5, 1942, Liz went into labor with her first child. Unfortunately, Ed was away on a mission in the Air Force, but her best friend, who lived next door, helped her get to the hospital. It was another unfortunate matter that the baby was born in a breach position, and the baby died. She was a full twelve pounds, but dead.

Liz dreaded telling Edward, and she wished that he had been there with her when it all happened. When she did tell him, he was sad, but he tried to encourage her not to worry for it was not her fault and he would get her pregnant again.

He sighed, "Maybe this baby just wasn't meant for this world, and God wanted her to be in heaven. We'll just have to be patient and keep on trying. When the time is right, we will have a child."

In September of 1942, Elizabeth was informed that she was pregnant again. Unfortunately, again, after having gone through the full nine month gestation period, she went into labor and this baby was also in a breach position and died. She was about one pound lighter than the first baby.

The tears of disappointment just lingered in both of their hearts. So much excitement and then such awful let downs. It's really hard to express how badly they both must have felt.

Arise Above All Disappointment

From all life's disappointments and fears, we certainly can't hide,
Unless we pray and trust in the Lord that He truly will provide.

Your richness in faith will grow as you learn
To depend on the Lord, ask Him for what you yearn.

Believe all things work together for those who love the Lord,
Get on your knees and pray with faith that God's true to His Word.

It's hard, I know, true to Jesus to be,
But a sweet savor imparts eventually.

A soul that is lost will eventually find,
The nurture of bliss is gone from the mind.

Live for love and prayer to the Lord,
And peace will surround you, in all accord.

Romans 8:24,25 ~ *For we are saved by hope: but hope that is seen is not hope: for what a man seeth why doth he yet hope for? But if we hope for that which we see not, then do we with patience wait for it.*

Isaiah 40:31 ~ *But they that wait upon the Lord shall renew their strength...*

A Baby is Born

It was March of 1944 when Elizabeth got pregnant for the third time. Of course, her fear of losing another baby had already been doubled. She tried to be very diligent to take every precaution and she prayed to the Lord to please let this baby live and be healthy. She was so sad and disappointed that she had lost her first two babies. Then, it was the Christmas season and the baby was due to be born in December that year. Could it be that her first child would be like a Christmas present of life?

On December 19, 1944, she had a nine pound, 5 ounce baby girl who lived, and the whole season was full of joy for Elizabeth and Edward.

With heartfelt tears of gratitude, Liz looked up to the doctor after being delighted by the sound of a healthy crying baby.

"Doctor! Is my baby going to live? Is she all right?"

"Oh yes. You have a healthy baby girl, and she is fine."

As the doctor went out to the waiting room, he saw Edward pacing up and down the hall and looking very worried.

"Doctor! Is Elizabeth all right? Did the baby live?"

"Come over here, son. Yes, your wife is fine and finally you and your wife are parents of a baby girl. I know it's been a very difficult time for both of you over the last number of years. It is such a gratifying feeling to have helped you both finally reach this goal, especially after having lost the first two babies."

"Thank you so much, Doctor."

"Liz," he said as he entered her room, "Oh Liz, I was praying for you and the baby and God does answer prayers."

"Ed, I'm so glad. I didn't think I was going to make it for a while there. Your prayers must have helped. I'd like to go out and shout this news to the world. I'm so excited! My daughter, Barbara Lynn Brennan lives! She lives! Praise the Lord!

Psalms 128:3 ~ *Thy wife shall be as a fruitful vine by the sides of thine house; thy children like olive plants round about thy table.*

Psalms 127:3 ~ *Lo, children are a heritage of the Lord: and the fruit of the womb is his reward.*

An Infant's Cry

Lift your arms up way high,
Have praise to Him above.

A new life is now in nigh,
A gift of God's true love.

Just a babe in a blanket sometime will be
A cause and a result for new history.

Millions of babies are born each day,
It's only God's creation in a glad foray.

Oh, the excitement and thrill to hear a newborn cry,
Then the chills of wonderment that tend to mystify.

It happens all the time; it's nothing new,
But these thoughts only come when it happens to you.

God tenderly molds every life to be,
He knows, from the first cry, all of its infirmities.

That first breath of air leads up to a frightful scream,
Joy fills the room; a new life is now in the mean.

Thank you, dear Lord, for this new love that I hold,
I'm caressing her body which my arms do unfold.

Help me to delight, even when she cries,
Just a little more patience and fewer sighs.

So fast a baby grows; treasure every year,
All in all there is no one so dear.

At times she may seem to be a little irritating,
But this is a miracle of God now slowly unfolding.

Just like a rose that is only a very tiny blossom,
In no time at all it will become a full bloom; isn't it
awesome?

Put not your hopes up only to despair,
All that's important is that you care.

Pray for her soul all that you can,
Teach from the Word; she'll soon understand.

Just be patient and prudent for her own sake,
Show love and affection, so she can partake

In the true love of Jesus which is shown in His Word.
Tell her that all throughout life, this she must learn.

Jeremiah 29:11 ~ *For I know the thoughts that I think toward you, saith the Lord, thoughts of peace, and not of evil, to give you an expected end.*

Jeremiah 29:12 ~ *Then shall ye call upon me, and ye shall go and pray unto me, and I will hearken to you.*

Deuteronomy 11:18,19 ~ *Therefore shall ye lay up these my words in your heart and in your soul, and bind them for a sign upon your hand, that they may be as frontlets between your eyes. And ye shall teach them your children, speaking of them when thou sittest in thine house, and when thou walkest by the way, and when thou liest down, and when thou risest up.*

Planting a Life Long Remembrance

After Edward had completed his full training session in San Francisco, he was transferred to an Air Force Base on the island of Hawaii. This occurred in 1945. Their stay was only to be for a short ten months and then Edward was transferred to Shaw Air Force Base in Greenville, South Carolina. Their place of living was off the base, out in the countryside. It was clearly a beautiful, country atmosphere compared to where they had previously been. The high humidity tendency sustained the rich green grass in the area, and the house had a white picket fence surrounding it.

It was during the spring of 1948, and Barbara was already three years old. She would always remember the time when she and her mother went out and planted pretty pansy flowers in front of the house. This young family of three just loved living there. Being in the country was a good and familiar atmosphere for Liz, and she kept herself busy by sewing all of her daughter's dresses and making curtains with her sewing machine. She was really a very good seamstress.

It's important to remember that little times of special togetherness with mother and child can have an impact that can last a lifetime.

Planting a Life Long Remembrance

I remember when I was only three,
My pretty Mom came up to me.

She said, "Come on, let's have some fun!
We'll go a planting, out in the sun."

My thoughts of wonderment were aroused.
It was Greenville, South Carolina where we were
housed.

"What is a planting?" I curiously said.
"It's putting plants in the flower bed," she said.

The sun was bright, the grass was green,
A white picket fence surrounded the scene.

I had never seen such a group of beautiful flowers,
As the pansies she had chosen in so many colors.

Mom dug little holes, not deep in the ground,
"What are you doing?" was my very first sound.

The pansies looked pretty in their little tiny pots.
"You must plant them in the ground, out of the pots."

I bet Mom never thought that I would remember,
That wonderful experience that continues to linger.

My favorite flowers still continue to be
The sweet fragile flower known as a pansy.

My mother was beautiful and strong like a rose.
I really didn't like roses; it's the thorns I suppose.

That day was vibrant, a few white clouds up above,
And this was an experience that forever I'd love.

Mother and daughter, so close we were,
Planting little flowers firm and secure.

Psalms 92:13-15 ~ *Those that be planted in the house of the Lord shall flourish in the courts of our God. They shall still bring forth fruit in old age; they shall be fat and flourishing; To shew that the Lord is upright: He is my rock, and there is no unrighteousness in Him.*

Illness, Stresses, and Another Move

During the winter of 1948, Elizabeth was overcome with pneumonia at least two different times. Her doctor in Greenville was quite worried about her. He stressed that these bouts of pneumonia might have a serious effect on her health.

Edward, having been promoted to Major in 1949, was transferred to Gunter Air Force Base in Montgomery, Alabama. Liz was so proud of Ed as he was going up in rank so speedily. She was assured that he was truly content being in the service of the Air Force. It was still very hard to think of moving from their little country home in Greenville, South Carolina, yet that is part of the reality of being in the service.

In the heat of the summer of 1949, Elizabeth prepared to move to Alabama. When they got there, it was quite a big readjustment to get used to living on the Gunter Air Force Base. Their quarters were small, but Elizabeth managed to make everything fit in and look homey. Elizabeth did have a knack for interior decorating.

During the time they lived in Alabama, there were three more times that Elizabeth came down with pneumonia. One of those times, she was diagnosed as having lobular pneumonia. Her doctor told her that she needed to go to a specialized hospital and have the lower right lobe of her lung removed. All of these bouts with pneumonia had damaged it so much that it was absolutely a necessity to have the operation, or she would eventually die from it.

By the year of 1951, Edward L. Brennan had achieved the rank of Lieutenant Colonel. It was during the end of April when he found out he needed to get a much needed transfer to Colorado for Elizabeth's health. Phitzimon's Army Hospital in Denver, Colorado was the suggested hospital for Liz to get her operation done. Fortunately he was able to pull some strings among the rank and files for this and managed to arrange for his transfer to Colorado Springs, which was about a half hour drive from Denver. The transfer would be in effect in July 1951.

1 Chronicles 16:11 ~ *Seek the Lord and his strength, seek his face continually.*

Isaiah 40:11 ~ *He shall feed his flock like a shepherd: he shall gather the lambs with his arm, and carry them in his bosom, and shall gently lead those that are with young.*

In the meantime, while still in Montgomery, Alabama, Liz was not feeling very strong. She would not admit this though. She knew that she had to pull herself up by the bootstraps and get everything ready to be moved within three months time. She was, of course, used to the moving process, but her weakness did make it very difficult for her. There are two qualities that she had that I did admire: her persistence and determination to face up to challenges and not to falter. She was not apt to give up on anything that she had to face in life.

Two weeks before the actual move, Ed had managed a one-week leave so that they could all go to the Gulf of Mexico near Pensacola, Florida. Oddly enough, when Ed told Liz about this leave he was taking, she was a little upset.

"Ed! We've got to move, and I need to pack all the breakable items, so they don't get broken," she cried.

"Elizabeth, I love you, and this is a very serious operation that you're going to have. I insist that we spend some good quality time together before you have this done!"

"Oh darling, I'll be all right. Don't you worry."

"Liz, I just couldn't live with myself if we don't take some time out for us to be together before this operation. Come on, both you and I could use a little vacation. I've reserved a little cottage which is right on the beach for us to spend our time together. I think you'll enjoy it."

"That does sound wonderful. Thank you, dear. You are so thoughtful and I do look forward to this."

"Now look, Liz, I want you to let the movers do the packing, so don't you bother about it. If anything breaks, we will replace it later. We desperately need this time together, and in the meantime, you must rest and get your strength."

"But I'm not tired."

"I insist, Liz. You know, I've been told that the sand on the Gulf beaches is as white as snow. You'll just love this little getaway. I've also been told that it is the season for the king crab to spawn. We can catch some and try cooking and eating them fresh from the ocean. Now, doesn't that sound like fun?"

"You're right, Ed. We may never have the opportunity to do this again. You are so thoughtful, dear. I really am looking forward to taking this trip. Thank you so much!"

When Elizabeth told little Barbara, then six years old, she got so very excited about going to see the ocean. Barbara had only seen pictures of the ocean before this. She remembered visiting her grandparents who lived in Palm Beach, Florida; but she only remembered going out to her grandpa's boat dock, not the beach front.

There is nothing so soothing as a nice little getaway to the ocean to help one be able to bear what might lie ahead.

The week in Pensacola was certainly one that would be remembered. The water was so clear and glassy, one could even see a tiny sand dollar lying in the white sand under three feet of water. The cabin was situated right along the beach side. It was the kind of vacation that one would dream of having. The time of year was just right for the large king crab to amble in towards the seashore to spawn, as the tide slowly rolled in.

Little Barbara had so much fun. She would walk down the coastline with her Mom and Dad, and she would look for and collect a variety of sea shells. Towards the end of the day, she went with them also to catch the large crabs. When she saw a crab for the first time she screamed in utter fright.

"Oh! Mommy, those look like big, ugly spiders! I don't like crabs at all."

"Don't worry, dear. Those are shellfish. Do you see the shells on their backs? That's why they are called shellfish. You see, I'll just boil them in a large pot and I'll fix deviled crab for dinner tonight."

"Oh no! Do you mean that we are going to eat those awful looking things?"

"Yes, dear, but we won't eat the shells. Just like we've eaten shrimp and oysters when we have gone out to dinner, we will eat these. You've just never seen a live shrimp or oyster. Now, don't you worry, I am sure that these will taste good."

Yes, she was right. From that time on, Barbara knew that her Mom was the best cook in the world.

James 1:2-4 ~ *My brethren, count it all joy when ye fall into divers temptations; Knowing this, that the trying of your faith worketh patience. But let patience have her perfect work, that ye may be perfect and entire, wanting nothing.*

The Sea of Life

The ocean is truly a wonderful place,
The tide rolls in and out at a steady pace.

To hear the sound of waves flowing and breaking,
Gives a quiet soul an almost new bright awakening.

It's God's reassurance that through life's many waves,
We'll always get by only through Jesus who saves.

Storms, though they send clouds and often affliction,
Strengthen our faith and love of Jesus without
remission.

Ofttimes I would take a trip to the ocean,
To relieve my mind of all the commotion.

From my mind, I peacefully think on,
And slowly set into quiet oblivion.

The world has come to have such a fast pace,
One needs a break to get out of this hectic race.

Jesus did walk on and by the ocean side,
Throughout my life, He's always my guide.

Psalms 119:92 ~ *Unless thy law had been my delight, I should then have perished in mine affliction.*

Psalms 119:105 ~ *Thy word is a lamp unto my feet, and a light unto my path.*

Rocks From Colorado

In June of 1951, Elizabeth and the family had just returned from their little vacation and she was hustling and bustling about the house to make sure that everything would be ready for the move to Colorado. Barbara rushed up to her.

"Mommy, why do we have to go to Colorado?"

"Well, Barbara, your daddy has been transferred to do his work in Colorado Springs."

"But why can't we move to Pensacola and live at the beach?"

"It's hard for me to explain, but your father is in the service of the U.S. Air Force; and wherever his superior officers tell him that he must go, he must go. I can tell you also that the beach is not always the safest place to live."

"Why not?"

"You will learn later in life that there are awful storms in the Gulf of Mexico and in Florida. They are called hurricanes. You can believe me that you wouldn't want to be caught in one of those storms."

"I still don't want to move. I will miss my friends and I don't want to be the new girl in class. It's awful! I know how the students at my school treat new kids in class."

Honey, it will be all right. I'll tell you another reason that we are going to Colorado is that I need to go to Phitzimmons Army Hospital so that I can have an operation on my lung. It's very important. Do you remember when you had an operation to remove your appendix? Well, that is similar to what I need to have."

"Oh, no! Mommy, will you be all right?"

"I'll be all right, honey. But do you know who to really look to and depend on to make everything all well and good?"

"Is it Jesus?"

"Yes, dear. Jesus will make all the decisions. Do you remember how I taught you to pray to Jesus every night before you go to sleep?"

"Do you mean, 'Now I lay me down to sleep, I pray the Lord my soul to keep. If I should die before I wake, I pray the Lord my soul to take'?"

"Yes, Barbara, and when you pray, you must also pray for others as well as yourself. Now, if you ever find yourself worrying, you must get on your knees and pray to the Lord. He will help all of His children, including you and anyone who lives. Even the people you may not like, you must pray for them. Remember that even before you were born, God had a plan for your whole life."

"But Mom, what if you die?"

"If I were to die, it would be just a part of God's plan for my life. But don't you worry, Barbara, I'll be just fine. Now, when you say your prayers, maybe you could say a little prayer for me. Jesus hears all of your prayers, even before you say them; and He will answer any prayer you ask. Here, listen to what it says in the Bible:

James 5:15 *...and the prayer of faith will save the sick.*"

"Thank you, Mommy. I will pray for you."

In July, 1951 the move to Colorado was not as difficult as it had been expected to be. The Brennan family didn't have to live on an Air Force Base which proved to be quite different and a lot more pleasant. The house they moved into was built on a slight hill. The front yard faced the beautiful valley of Colorado Springs and a mountain which is called Cheyenne Mountain, a part of the Rocky Mountain range. At the bottom of this long half-pyramid shaped mountain was the Biltmore Hotel which has a very large skating rink inside of it. Here is where professional ice skaters come to put on the most exhilarating shows on ice.

About 45 degrees around the house from the front, one could see the majestic Rocky Mountains, including the well known Pike's Peak which is 14,110 feet high into the sky. This was such a beautiful place to live; just the sight of those mountains was breathtaking to anyone's eyes. This sight could make one wonder in awe and thankfulness for God's creation of such a beautiful earth.

For some reason, Barbara decided that she was going to be a rock collector, and her mother encouraged her by bringing her two pretty rocks one day.

"I've got something for you, Barbara. Here is a turquoise rock and a clear quartz rock. How do you like them?"

"Oh, those are so pretty! One looks almost like glass. I've never seen any rocks that were so clear."

"Here is another one that is called topaz."

"That's pretty, but I don't like the orange color of it. Thank you, Mom. I am going to see if I can find some more rocks like these."

Elizabeth went to Phitzimmon's Army Hospital which was located near Denver. She was there for two weeks having her long-dreaded surgery. The lower right lobe of her lung needed to be removed before infection would spread. Although it was a very painful surgery, it was a successful one.

While Liz was in the hospital, Edward made sure to keep Barbara involved with her rock collecting so as not to let her sit around worrying about her Mom. He took her several places, even to a rock quarry, so that she might find more rocks for her little collection. This was so thoughtful of Ed. They were good and meaningful times that Barbara spent with her Dad. Of course, they would go and visit Elizabeth as soon as she could have visitors.

When Ed would take Barbara in the car to Denver, it was about an hour drive. Before visiting the hospital, he would take Barbara to a place just outside of Denver called Red Rock. There she would climb around looking for rocks. It's not easy to find a really good rock in this earth. If one looks to the Lord, though, he'll find the best rock of all:

2 Samuel 22:2,3 *And he said, The Lord is my rock, and my fortress, and my deliverer; The God of my rock; in him will I trust: he is my shield, and the horn of my salvation, my high tower, and my refuge, my saviour; thou savest me from violence.*

God Is My Rock

Give to me confidence that I might enjoy,
The rock of God which no one can destroy.

A life of perfect security in thee,
The Lord and His Word all satisfy me.

A diamond is beautiful, and as hard as it is,
God is my sure rock; He won't set my heart amiss.

The quarry of all life, created by God,
Is only upheld by the mountain of God.

He is our fortress, blade, and shield.
The light of his love is often revealed.

Remember that the Lord is the horn of salvation,
And He is the refuge that prevents violation.

Praise the Lord for being your rock.
Just pray, and He will hear your gentle knock.

Through the "valley of the shadow of death,"
His spirit will lead you along the right path.

If you love Him with all mind, soul, and heart,
He'll help you and comfort you and never depart.

1 Corinthians 10:4 ~ *And did all drink the same spiritual drink: for they drank of that spiritual Rock that followed them: and that Rock was Christ.*

Edward tried to encourage Barbara.

"Barbara, you remember the song that we sang in church called 'Rock of Ages,' don't you?"

"Yes, Daddy."

"Here is another song about Jesus who is our rock. I want you to learn this and remember it. Okay?"

My hope is built on nothing less,
Than Jesus' blood and righteousness,
I dare not trust the sweetest frame,
But wholly lean on Jesus' name.

When darkness seems to hide His face,
I rest on His unchanging grace,
In every high and stormy gale
My anchor holds within His veil.

On Christ, the Solid Rock I stand
All other ground is sinking sand
All other ground is sinking sand.

Lyrics written by Edward Mote
Hymn: My Hope Is Built on Nothing Less
2002 Frankie's Farm Music

Psalms 18:1, 2 ~ *I will love thee, O Lord, my strength. The Lord is my rock, and my fortress, and my deliverer; my God, my strength, in whom I will trust; my buckler and the horn of my salvation, and my high tower.*

Patience to Endure

Although still in pain, Elizabeth was released from the hospital just two weeks after the operation to remove the lower right lobe of her lung. She truly missed being at home with her husband and daughter. Her pain was so bad that she needed pain pills, but was very cautious not to use them unless it was absolutely necessary. Even though the pain was excruciating, she kept herself strong and endured this all with little or no complaints. She prayed often to the Lord to relieve her and she found comfort. One of her prayers might have been like this:

Though illness may strike,
I do not fear,
For my Lord above,
He is always near.

Upset and in pain,
I won't complain.
Fret not I,
For Jesus sustains.

I need His strength
Throughout each day,
To surmount my weakness and
Make me whole always.

93

Let my voice
Linger not in woe.
I must rejoice,
For He told me so.

The Spirit of God makes intercession,
And takes away all of my oppression.

Romans 8:26 ~ *Likewise the Spirit also helpeth our infirmities: for we know not what we should pray for as we ought: but the Spirit itself maketh intercession for us with groanings which cannot be uttered.*

Psalms 73:26 ~ *My flesh and my heart faileth: but God is the strength of my heart, and my portion for ever.*

North to Alaska

Elizabeth, after nine months of recovery from her lung surgery, was so surprised when Edward came home and told her that he had received new orders to be transferred in the summer of 1952 to Elmendorf Air Force Base in Anchorage, Alaska.

"Oh, Ed! I can't go through another move now! Why is this happening so soon?"

"Liz, this transfer we had to Colorado Springs was a very temporary one, so that you could be operated on at Phitzimmon's Army Hospital. Remember?"

"I am sorry, honey. I just can't believe that we have to pack up and leave Colorado so soon. I really love it here."

"I do too, Liz."

One thing about being in the service was that, at any time, one could be transferred to any place in the world, depending on where one was needed. It all depended on the senior officers in charge.

Liz was so fragile that she couldn't be hugged the way Ed would have done normally. So he just looked at her with loving eyes and held her hand gently to try to reassure her.

"Liz, I'll take care of the move. You can rely on me. This will be easy, and I want you to have nothing to do with getting things together for this move. Please, just let me handle this. Okay?"

This move would not be difficult because many of the items in the house had been left packed from the previous move. At the time, World War II had, of course, ended, but the 'cold' war with Korea was in effect. Also, Alaska was one of the U.S. territories, not yet officially a state.

Since Ed happened to be a member of the American Automobile Association, he was able to get a whole route mapped out for them to travel from Colorado Springs to Seattle, Washington. It was referred to as the 'northern route.' This would be a very scenic route to travel.

"Elizabeth, look! We'll be able to go to Yellowstone National Park. We'll see the Grand Teton National Park as well. All along this route, we will see the Rocky Mountains. Doesn't that sound wonderful?"

"But Ed, isn't that going to be a very long drive for you?"

"Oh, that doesn't matter. This is a great opportunity. It'll be worth it to me. Believe me, it will be a good trip. Wait and see. Although it is a long drive, we will get to see sights that we may never get a chance to see again. The sight of the Old Faithful geyser and all the other geysers and all the mountainous regions will make this trip almost like a vacation for us."

While traveling this route, they did enter both of the parks that he had told her about. Elizabeth remarked how beautiful the mountains were.

"Mommy, why do you think that mountains are so beautiful? They just look like rocks and dirt to me."

"Let me tell you, young lady, these are a part of God's creation, and we should thank the Lord for this beautiful earth."

"I guess you are right. I'm glad you gave me my Brownie camera so I could take pictures."

"There is one more thing that you will understand as you get older. Mountains are like life's challenges. You climb and climb to get to the top, and once you've reached the top, it's an easy ride down the mountain."

"Hmm, I think I understand."

"Here is a verse from the Bible that would be good for you to try to memorize:
Matthew 17:20 ~ *And Jesus said unto them, 'Because of your unbelief: for verily I say unto you, If ye have faith as a grain of mustard seed, ye shall say unto this mountain, Remove hence to yonder place; and it shall remove; and nothing shall be impossible unto you.'"*

The Beauty of the Earth

On restless days, I'd slow myself down,
To gaze at the beauty of the earth all around.

The flutter of a bird, gently landing
On the branch of a tree firmly standing.

On the ground which God created that way,
Delights my soul to look up, smile, and say,

"Lord you are so kind and so extremely powerful,
You've given such beauty and You are so thoughtful."

Care not we, while we're so in a hurry,
To render thankfulness and be merry.

Life goes on, as we would say,
God made earth in just two days.

Some mountains are high and hard to climb,
But love in the Lord gives life ease all the time.

Jesus forgives us and loves us with His grace,
So we need not climb mountains at a very fast pace.

Just relax and see all the beautiful trees,
This will truly make you feel quite at ease.

Don't make a mountain out of a mole hill, I've been told,
Ask Jesus to help you; He'll make you to feel bold.

The mountains I've seen are filled with pines,
Birds go a winging, all different kinds.

Faith, as a grain of a mustard seed, in the Bible I read
Can even move a large mountain from its stead.

The earth is so beautiful, the land is so vast,
My soul is comforted, finally at last.

Psalms 33:4, 5 ~ *For the word of the Lord is right; and all his works are done in truth. He loveth righteousness and judgment: the earth is full of the goodness of the Lord.*

Psalms 65:5-7,9,10,13 ~ *By terrible things in righteousness wilt thou answer us, O God of our salvation; who art the confidence of all the ends of the earth, and of them that are afar off upon the sea: Which by His strength setteth fast the mountains; being girded with power: Which stilleth the noise of the seas, the noise of their waves, and the tumult of the people. Thou visiteth the earth and waterest it:*

thou greatly enrichest it with the river of God, which is full of water: thou preparest them corn, when thou hast so provided for it. Thou waterest the ridges thereof abundantly: thou settlest the furrows thereof: thou makest it soft with showers: thou blessest the springing thereof. The pastures are clothed with flocks; the valleys also are covered over with corn; they shout for joy, they also sing.

Alaska, the New Frontier

When the Brennan family finally reached Seattle, Washington, they knew that they must get the proper clothing for living so close to the arctic circle. One would not just wear a heavy overcoat in that region to stay warm. In Seattle, there were many places to get fur parkas, fur scarfs, leather gloves, ear muffs, boots, thermal underwear, and so many other things that would be needed to survive the bitter cold winters. It was best to buy these things in Seattle because otherwise one would have to buy them for a much higher price in Alaska. Remember that Alaska was still a new frontier at the time, and there weren't many department stores there yet.

In August of 1952, Ed, Liz, and Barbara boarded a large ocean liner at the Seattle Sea Port. The boat was very large, and it was a necessity to have plenty of Dramamine to fight off sea sickness.

"Mommy, why do I feel like I need to throw up?"

"Barbara, you are seasick. Here, take one of these and you will feel better."

"What is seasick?"

"It has to do with the change in gravity that comes about when you are in a boat that is floating on the water. This happens in other places like in an airplane and even sometimes in a car. Don't get yourself in a tiff, everyone gets this. Come here, let's go out and see if we can see some whales."

"Whales?"

"Come on. I'll show you. You'll like this."

What an amazing sight to see such long and large fish just swimming about and spewing water from their spouts very high in the air.

This boat took them to a well known port called Seward, Alaska. It was also said to be an ice free port at the gateway of Alaska. Seward certainly was not a beautiful city like Seattle was. It was located at a large fishing marina where many fishing boats were docked. Many were coming and going throughout the day. Seward was named for former Secretary of State, William Seward, who arranged for the purchase of Alaska in 1867.

The time of year was, of course, fall. During the fall and the spring equinoxes, a colorful natural light show appears way up in the sky. This is known as the Aurora Borealis. This wonderful sight was something to look forward to in this area of Alaska which was so close to the North Pole.

The trip from Seward to Anchorage was a very overwhelming sight to see. The Brennans finally got to Elmendorf Air Force Base and settled into their quarters on the base. Unlike other quarters that they had lived in previously, this was a two-story house with a large two car garage located underneath the house.

Thanksgiving arrived, and later, the snow began to fall. There are often high winds that come along with blizzards. It is understood that the wind gets so strong that it can blow up to the speed of 115 miles per hour.

It is also understood that from January through March, the temperatures drop as cold as 20-30 degrees below zero. Also, parts of Alaska can receive 20 feet of snow per year.

Lt. Colonel Edward Brennan was promoted to the rank of Full Colonel and was a pilot in the Air Force by now. He was 36 years old, which was quite young for reaching this rank. Again, Liz was so proud of him, but she realized that his being in the service at this rank was becoming a political strain on him. It was putting Edward under quite a bit of stress.

Psalms 39:13 ~ *O spare me, that I may recover strength, before I go hence, and be no more.*

A New Horizon

Alaska, Alaska, what do I see?
A land so vast and a new frontier to me.

Your mountains so high and land so fertile,
Mt. McKinley stands so far up and seems so virile.

The snow gently falls and sets upon the ground,
Such a peaceful grandeur I've never found.

There's a noise in my head or a ringing in my ear,
What's written in God's Word is so perfectly clear.

A new horizon of life seems to always begin,
When we open our hearts and ask Jesus to come in.

This blanket of snow is so white, I would say
I wonder if in heaven it could be that way.

We're washed with the blood, how pure and so fine,
Is the precious Lord Jesus Christ, the Divine.

How fortunate am I to see such a scene,
Of a land covered in white, looking so keen.

Alaska, Alaska, you look like a dream.

From Death To Life Everlasting

On February 5, 1954, the Brennans had been in Alaska for approximately one-and-a-half years. Edward was ordered to go out on a mission which was to be located in the northern Alaskan skies and told Elizabeth little about it. He had been on many missions before this one, but Liz had thoughts about this one which she explained.

"Ed, I heard on the radio that there's going to be a very large blizzard in just the area that you are going. Please, there must be some mistake that they are sending you there at this time."

"Aw, Liz, there are blizzards all the time up here. Don't worry. My senior officers know what they are doing."

"Oh, Ed! My instincts just tell me that you shouldn't go!"

"I love you, honey. Nothing will go wrong, I promise you. You'll see me back here in just a few days. You know I must do what my commander tells me to do. Just don't worry, darling."

It is so very unfortunate that the unease Elizabeth felt about this impending mission was about to be realized.

In the early morning of the very snowy day, February 6, 1954, Elizabeth was visited by the Base Commander. She was told that Ed's plane had blown up while he was flying in some desolate region of northern Alaska.

She was so overcome with grief at the fact that her beloved husband was dead. Elizabeth had faced the death of her own mother when she was only nine years old, and now this had to happen. It was like history was repeating itself.

The agony and grief that Liz felt was so overwhelming, and now she had to relay this horrible news to her own daughter. She wiped away her tears, and she thought of the Bible which says that everything happens for a reason. This helped her get a grasp on herself.

After she had composed herself, she picked up her Bible and went ahead bravely to her daughter's room. It was approximately 6:45am and Barbara was getting ready to go to school.

"Barbara, I need for you to sit down and talk to me for a minute. First, let's pray the Lord's prayer that I taught you."

"Okay, Mommy, I'll pray with you."

"Our Father which art in heaven, hallowed be thy name. Thy kingdom come. Thy will be done in earth, as it is in heaven. Give us this day our daily bread, and forgive us our debts, as we forgive our debtors. And lead us not into temptation, but deliver us from evil: For thine is the kingdom, and the power, and the glory forever. Amen."

"Mom, what's going on?"

"I'm sorry to tell you at such a young age about this, but did you know that I was speaking to some men at the front door just a few minutes ago? Well, they came to deliver some bad news to me, and now I must tell you about it."

"What is this, Mom? What happened?"

"Barbara, Daddy died in an airplane crash..."

"No! No! No! Nooooo! Daddy didn't die, did he?"

"Yes, child. Darling, I'm so sorry to tell you this."

"Mom, this is so bad! I just can't take it!"

"Barbara, go ahead and cry. You need to."

"I just can't believe you!"

"It's true, dear."

"Why did God take away my daddy, Mommy? I love him so much. I just can't go on living without him."

"Honey, you'll see that many things that happen in life are hard to understand, but in the Bible it is written in Romans 8:28: *And we know that all things work together for good to them that love God, to them who are called according to his purpose.*

"I still don't understand, Mom. Why? Why? Why?"

"I'm sorry Barbara. You know, we are going to be all right. Just let your tears out, and you and I will be just fine. You see, even before we are babies inside of our mother's womb, God has made a plan for our whole life through."

"He does? You mean He knows everything that is going to happen in our lives before it happens?"

"Yes, dear. He does, and we need not be afraid."

Both mother and daughter were in a state of shock, and they both were weeping. It was just a few minutes later that the Base Chaplain came to speak to both Elizabeth and her daughter about the loss of Edward Brennan.

"Mrs. Brennan, I'm so sorry for the pain you and your daughter must be feeling at this time. I just thought I might be able to soothe your thoughts a little. You do understand that you and I and all of mankind are children of God, don't you?"

"Of course."

"Let me say that we must learn to accept the fact that God is in control, and as unfortunate as this is, you must not resent the Lord for your loss. That would be selfish. You see, life is a process through which we must learn to not just love things and relationships in this world. We must learn daily to love and honor the Lord God who has all control of everything that is in heaven and earth."

"Chaplain, if God loves us as His children, then why does He bring such grief to my heart?"

"Barbara, God didn't kill your daddy. The plane he was flying in just blew up and killed him, but his soul is alive in heaven with the Lord. You'll probably live a lot longer, but someday, you will see your daddy in heaven with God. You see, life on this earth is like a small breeze. In heaven, you will see forever, if you'll only love the Lord with all your heart, soul, mind, and might. Do you know the verse in the Bible about that?"

"Well, my Mommy told me something about that."

"Luke 10:27 says: *And he answering said, 'Thou shalt love the Lord thy God with all thy heart, and with all thy soul, and with all thy strength, and with all thy mind; and thy neighbor as thyself.'* Now, I want you to try to memorize this and think of it all the time, and pray to the Lord. He will help you and your Mom. Mrs. Brennan, I assure you that the Air Force will help you to get to Arlington National Cemetery, and we will arrange the move and the storage that you'll need until you are finally relocated to wherever you decide to settle down."

"Thank you so much, Chaplain. Your visit is much appreciated and thank you for all the reassurance."

1 John 3:19, 20 ~ *And hereby we know that we are of the truth, and shall assure our hearts before him. For if our heart condemns us, God is greater than our heart, and knoweth all things.*

O Divine Master, grant that I may not so much seek
To be consoled as to console;
To be understood as to understand;
To be loved as to love;
For it is in giving that we receive;
It is in pardoning that we are pardoned;
It is in dying that we are born to eternal life!

From the Prayer of St. Francis

Be Thou my vision, O Lord of my heart;
Naught be all else to me, save that Thou art--
Thou my best thought, by day or by night,
Waking or sleeping, Thy presence my light.

Be thou my wisdom, and Thou my true Word;
I ever with Thee and Thou with me, Lord;
Thou my great Father, I Thy true son,
Thou in me dwelling, and I with Thee one.

Riches I heed not, nor man's empty praise,
Thou mine inheritance, now and always;
Thou and only Thou, first in my heart,
High King of heaven, my treasure Thou art.

Traditional hymn from Ireland,
Author unknown

A New Beginning

After the chaplain left, Liz went in directly to talk to Barbara. Courageously, Liz took her daughter in her arms to comfort her.

"God loves you, Barbara. Everything will be all right. You'll see. Now, let's get on our knees and pray to the Lord Jesus, and ask him to help us both to just get through this. He will hear our prayers, and He will help us both. Just have faith and hope in the Lord. You know, after my Mom died, when I was your age, I learned to depend on Jesus every day that I lived by praying and reading the Bible. He does hear your every prayer, and you will be comforted by the Holy Spirit. You know that Daddy wants us to be happy again and thankful to the Lord that he is in heaven now."

"But I want him here!"

"Here's a verse from the Bible that I want you to learn and then memorize. Okay?"

"Oh, all right."

"Matthew 26:39 says: *And he went a little further, and fell on his face, and prayed, saying, 'O my Father, if it be possible, let this cup pass from me: nevertheless not as I will, but as thou wilt.'* That means that no matter what happens, it's not always what we want, but rather, it is what God decides for us that we must follow. Proverbs 20:24 says: *Man's*

112

goings are of the Lord; how can a man understand his own way?"

"Really?"

"Yes, Barbara. You see, God had a plan for your whole life, even before you were born."

"You've told me that before. Does it say that in the Bible?"

"Yes, it does. Here, I'll read it to you from Ephesians 1:11. *In whom also we have obtained an inheritance, being predestined according to the purpose of him who worketh all things after the counsel of his own will.*"

"This is hard, Mommy."

"I know, but we must always seek the strength of the Lord to help us to pull through it all. He will help us. Just believe in the Lord, and He will make a way for us."

Psalms 146:9 ~ *The Lord preserveth the strangers; he relieveth the fatherless and widow; but the way of the wicked he turneth upside down.*

Psalms 71:6 ~ *By thee have I been holden up from the womb: thou art he that took me out of my mother's bowels: my praise shall be continually of thee.*

God's Will Be Done

Before I was born, and before my first cry,
God had predestined my life; now I must try

To flow as a river down my life's path,
To think not of myself and remember God's wrath.

We need not to fret each day as we live,
For the Lord is gracious, and He does forgive.

The Lord is so good, and you will find,
None is so loving, so comforting and kind.

Help me Lord more to understand,
I need but to ask for your loving hand.

When the river becomes rough and the rocks you must
mind,
Give in to the Lord, for your life is already pre-
aligned.

Entrust your thoughts and fears to Him as you pray,
He surely will comfort and lead you not astray.

Though, as hard as it seems, my mind must admit,
Life can be beautiful while you depend on the Spirit.

He'll comfort and clean you from the dirt and the grit,
Ask for His refuge, and you He will not omit.

A little prayer of faith from you in love,
And He'll answer all prayers from high above.

Psalms 46:1,2 ~ *God is our refuge and strength, a very present help in trouble. Therefore will not we fear, though the earth be removed, and though the mountains be carried into the midst of the sea.*

James 4:14,15 ~ *Whereas ye know not what shall be on the morrow. For what is your life? It is even a vapour, that appeareth for a little time, and then vanisheth away. For that ye ought to say, If the Lord will, we shall live, and do this, or that.*

Life Rearranged

Elizabeth knew that this was a time for the renewing of her spirit, and that she would have to depart from the past. She was so courageous about the daunting changes that she would have to adjust to.

Fortunately, Edward left her an adequate amount of money through the insurance policy, and veterans benefits, and she would have access to any military base for medical benefits. These benefits she would surely need, having a child to bring up and keep healthy. She was, in 1953, thirty-five years of age; and with no previous work experience she would have a very hard time finding a job to support herself and her young child alone, without some help.

Her faith was strong, and though she felt as if she were broken in half, she turned to pray to the Lord for His strength and guidance to help her to go on in this world alone.

Luke 4:18 ~ *...He hath sent me to heal the brokenhearted, to preach deliverance to the captives, ...to set at liberty them that are bruised.*

Arrangements were made for Elizabeth and her daughter to be flown to Richmond, Virginia, to be with her father at Arlington National Cemetery in Washington D.C. which is very close to Springhill Farm. Arlington National Cemetery is where Barbara's father, Colonel Edward Longfellow

Brennan was to be buried with full honors for being a Korean war hero.

Evan went to the airport to pick up his daughter and his granddaughter. As he was searching for them, he spotted them sitting in the coffee shop and rushed up to them in the excitement of just seeing them again, after so long not seeing them.

"Elizabeth! Oh, Elizabeth! I found you! Are you all right? I'm so sorry about the loss of your husband. Come here, sweetheart. Let me hold you and hug you."

"Don't worry, Dad. We got here about twenty minutes ago, and I just decided that we would stop here for a little something to eat. Dad, I'll be all right. I just have to figure out where I'm going and what I'm going to do next, now that Ed is gone. I'm so glad and relieved to have you near me now during this awful travail."

Psalms 31:24 ~ *Be of good courage, and he shall strengthen your heart, all ye that hope in the Lord.*

"Come on. Let's go to Springhill Farm. Merlinda, my cook and housekeeper, has prepared a nice brunch for us all. You can stay at Springhill for as long as you need to get readjusted. The fact is you could move in and stay with me for as long as you like. You do know that you are always welcome to come home, don't you?"

"Yes, Dad. Thank you very much. I do need you right now. I don't think I had better move in, though. I feel compelled to get out in this world and make a new start in life. I hope that you understand what I mean by that."

"Liz, you have quite a challenge and many decisions to make. Just feel free to take your time at home. Okay?"

After making the funeral arrangements, Elizabeth made sure to lighten the load by taking Barbara to see all the historical memorials in Arlington and then to a beautiful art museum in Washington, D.C. This cheered up Barbara and was an experience to be treasured by both of them for many years.

Edward Longfellow Brennan's funeral was certainly a very honorable one, and Elizabeth accepted the American flag, though she had a hard time holding back her tears. She tried desperately to hold her own for the sake of Barbara, who was quite frightened by the 21 gun salute. She was also thankful that, when she would die, she could be buried right next to her husband, whom she so adored.

At the funeral was one of Edward's sisters, Cornelia. She had come all the way to Washington D. C. to be there. She invited Liz to bring her daughter, Barbara, to come down and stay for a while at her home in Jacksonville, Florida.

"Come on, Liz. You need a big change and some time to think things out. Barbara should get back to school where I am a teacher. You won't have to worry about your daughter, and you can stay for as long as you want to."

"Maybe you're right. I do need to get my daughter back in school. While I love my Dad, and he offered me the option to stay here, I would really prefer to be in a warmer climate. Thank you, Cornelia, I believe that I will take you up on your kind offer."

A few days after the funeral, Liz and her daughter were given air travel to Jacksonville, Florida by way of Air Force carrier. They stayed for approximately three weeks, and then Liz decided to call her Uncle Tom and Aunt Elinore in Pasadena, California. She asked if it would be all right for her to bring Barbara and stay until she would get settled down in southern California. Liz had been told by her doctors that she should live in a drier climate than Florida. This necessity was due to her lung problem. Her decision was final. She had made up her mind that she would go to Southern California to live.

Of course it was fortunate that the Jorgansens were more than happy to accommodate Elizabeth and Barbara.

Liz explained her intentions and thanked Cornelia for helping her and Barbara so much. Then, since she was still a member of the American Automobile Association, her long trip to California was mapped out for her.

It took about seven days to drive this distance by car. It was certainly worth all the hassle to Liz and she felt that she had made the right decision about where to settle down, though she still had to decide just where in Southern California she would finally relocate.

Realign My Life

Refresh my steps, as I continue on,
To realign my life upon this new dawn.

The Lord is my shepherd, watching over us all,
Making sure to redeem us before we would fall.

Again, I say, "Humble your heart to kneel down and
pray,
He'll comfort and guide you all of the way."

If a dark cloud appears out of the blue,
He'll help you to see a better point of view.

After all, each new day is yet to be embraced,
With cheerfulness of heart towards the past we have
faced.

Every link of time is embossed with times of trial,
Which fortifies our faith and helps us all the while.

To those who suffer pain, and to those who suffer
most,
You are merely the endearment of the silent Holy
Ghost.

It's a time to be grateful and hope to gratify
The Lord of creation who left His Word to testify,

That our personal obligation on this earth and in this life,
Is to intensify our love of God with all our heart, soul, and might.

Many souls are shallow and don't appreciate,
The very breath they take is up to God's mandate.

Impressed upon our heart should be His Holy Word,
That many, in this world, have never even heard.

You are one of those of which He did choose,
To be a soldier of God and you will never lose.

You need not be in a hurry; stop and take a rest,
Think of what Jesus would do, for He knows what's best.

Proverbs 3:5-7 *Trust in the Lord with all thine heart; and lean not unto thine own understanding. In all thy ways acknowledge him, and he shall direct thy paths. Be not wise in thine own eyes: fear the Lord, and depart from evil.*

A Fresh Start in California

It was the early part of April of 1954 when Elizabeth with her daughter, Barbara, arrived in Pasadena, California at the Jorgansen's home. Right away, Elizabeth made sure to get Barbara back into school. She chose a Catholic school because she knew that the sisters would be attentive to Barbara and she mentioned to them the problem she had with resentment towards God for taking her father away. Hopefully, they could help her to understand.

"I don't know what else to do, Aunt Elinore, I've got to find a place to settle down. I don't mean that I want to live with you. I need to figure out where I am going."

"Liz, I have a friend who is a real estate broker. I'll call her and ask her to come over here tomorrow. She'll be able to help you the best, I am sure."

"Thank you so much. I didn't think about talking to a real estate person. That's it! That is a great idea!"

One thing Liz had already decided was that she didn't want to live in Los Angeles or its suburbs. After discussing real estate objectives of Southern California with the broker at length, Liz decided to go with her to check out a house in Riverside. Liz had decided also that she would rent a house in Riverside, and later, she would look for a house there to buy.

"Mommy, where are we going to live? I really would like it if we could stay here with Uncle Tom and Aunt Elinore."

"I know you like it here, Barbara, but we can't stay here. I've decided that we are going to move to a really nice house in Riverside. I like Riverside and I think you will too. Also, we'll be able to go to March Air Force Base if we need anything."

"Where is Riverside?"

"It's just about an hour's drive from here. Don't you worry, we'll be able to come here to visit during the holiday season. Your cousins will only be here at that time anyway."

Elizabeth and Barbara stayed with the Jorgansens until Barbara finished fourth grade in school. Then, in June of 1954, they moved to Riverside, California.

Riverside was only approximately twenty-five miles from March Air Force Base, so during the summer, Liz and her daughter would go there to the swimming pool, which was located at the Officer's Club. Occasionally, they would go out for dinner at the Club's dining room.

While living in a two-bedroom house located on the outskirts of Riverside, Elizabeth made sure to get Barbara involved in as many activities outside of school that she could, such as Brownies, piano lessons, camping, and the learning of how to keep up a house, including cooking and sewing. Of course they would participate together in household duties. In the meantime, Liz would go out searching for the right house to buy. She had to hurry in her search, but did want to be careful, for the house she would buy would end up being their final home.

"Mommy, it's so hard, moving from one place to another. Every time I would make a good friend who I enjoyed being with, we would then up and move away. I miss my friends. It's so disappointing."

"I understand, Sweetheart, but after I find the house I'm going to buy, this time we won't be moving anymore. In fact, I'm seriously considering one house in particular right now."

"Where is it? Will you show it to me?"

"Well, I'm really not positive that I'm going to get this one yet, but yes, I'll take you over to see it."

It was still the summer of 1954, and Riverside was just beginning to flourish. In the center of the city was its main attraction: the Mission Inn, which was, at one time, a beautiful large Spanish Mission. It took up the area of one city block and had been converted into a lavish hotel. It was also used as a community center for extravagant occasions.

The main street in Riverside, was Magnolia Boulevard, which was named for all the magnolia trees there along the side and in the center divider of the boulevard.

Elizabeth was driving down Magnolia Boulevard and, as they got further out of the center of the city and closer to where the house she was considering buying was, Barbara finally noticed that there was something in the trees.

"Mommy! Look! Those trees have really large flowers on them. I've never seen such huge flowers in my life!"

"They are beautiful, aren't they? Wait until you see the house."

The house was located at the end of a large cul-de-sac of homes on Rockingham Place. This area was largely residential, and there were schools within walking distance. Oddly enough, there was a large walnut tree in the center of the really large driveway, and all over the area were walnut trees. This area surely had been a walnut grove at one time.

After Elizabeth had taken Barbara inside the house and had driven her around the area, Liz wanted to see if her daughter was impressed.

"Now that I've shown you the house and the schools here, what do you think?" asked Elizabeth.

"I like it, Mommy," Barbara replied.

"Well, I believe my decision is final then. I've been considering this house for the last month and we are going to move in next month, just before school starts.

Psalms 30:4-6 ~ *Sing unto the Lord, O ye saints of his, and give thanks at the remembrance of his holiness. For his anger endureth but a moment; in his favour is life: weeping may endure for a night, but joy cometh in the morning. And in my prosperity I said, I shall never be moved.*

Settling Down

Having settled down finally in their new home, Liz and her daughter felt secure and happy there. In the summertime Liz continued to take Barbara to go swimming at the base pool. Elizabeth was a wonderful swimmer. She started to teach Barbara how to swim when Barbara was only three years old, so she was quite a good swimmer too. They both would go to the pool at the Officer's Club at least three days a week, and they would stay until it closed at 6:00pm. This was an invigorating way to get rid of the loneliness that lurked inside both of them; and it was also a good way to meet new friends and stay cool on the hot summer days.

Being a fan of the great actress and swimmer, Esther Williams, when the fancy, Esther Williams swimsuits came out on the market, Liz just had to have one. She had a beautiful figure and looked great in a swimsuit.

Once or twice a month, Liz would take Barbara to Laguna Beach. In fact, the beach became a favorite place to go.

"You know what, Barbara? The ocean beaches are so wondrous and ever changing. Did you know that Jesus used to walk along the beach by the Sea of Galilee?"

"Really? He was a beachcomber like you and me are?"

"Well, I'm not sure about that, but a friend of mine did tell me a story called 'Footprints in the Sand.' Here is how it goes:

One night, a man had a dream. He dreamed he was walking along the beach with the Lord. Across the sky flashed scenes from his life. For each scene, he noticed footprints in the sand: one belonging to him and the other to the Lord.

When the last scene of his life flashed before him, he looked back at the footprints in the sand. He noticed many times, along the path of his life, there was only one set of footprints. He also noticed that it happened at the very lowest and saddest times in his life.

This really bothered him, and he questioned the Lord about it. 'Lord, you said that once I decided to follow you, you'd walk with me all the way, but I have noticed that during the most troublesome times of my life, there is only one set of footprints in the sand. I don't understand why, when I needed you most, you would leave me?'

The Lord replied, 'My precious, precious child, I love you and I would never leave you. During your times of trial and suffering, when you only see one set of footprints, it was then that I carried you.' (Author unknown)"

"Is this really true, Mommy?"

"It is true that Jesus is always with you, even though His footprints are not showing. Also, He does love you and He will never leave you."

Hosea 1:10 ~ *Yet the number of the children of Israel shall be as the sand of the sea, which cannot be measured nor numbered; and it shall come to pass, that in the place where it was said unto them, Ye are not my people, there it shall be said unto them... Ye are the sons of the living God.*

John 7:1 ~ *After these things Jesus walked in Galilee: for he would not walk in Judaea, because the Jews sought to kill him.*

Matthew 8:25, 26 ~ *And his disciples came to him, and awoke him, saying, Lord, save us: we perish. And he saith unto them, "Why are ye so fearful, O ye of little faith?" Then He arose, and rebuked the winds and the sea; and there was a great calm.*

By The Sea

The ocean breeze fills me so,
As I walk upon the sand.
It seems the waves evenly flow,
And gently, He takes my hand.

It makes my heart so full of joy,
Just knowing that He is here.
No more will I be subtle and coy,
For with Him, I have no fear.

See the shells, tossed to and fro,
As the sand cuddles my feet.
And in His path, I intend to go,
With no suffering or defeat.

Oh, the beauty of an ocean sunset,
With shimmering colors in the sky,
Dazzles me so, I will never fret,
No more will I need to cry.

Psalms 77:19 ~ *Thy way is in the sea, and thy path in the great waters, and thy footsteps are not known.*

Life Goes On

Elizabeth and Barbara had a favorite church which they attended every Sunday morning. One particular Sunday, they went to join the members for a brunch which was held after the early morning service. They were patiently waiting for the waitress to come when one of the members came over to sit at the table with them.

"May I join you? I don't want you to be all alone," he said.

"Of course. That would be fine," replied Liz.

"I'm Randy Weekly. I've seen you before at church, but I've never had the pleasure of meeting you."

Liz and Barbara got to know Randy. He was a lawyer who practiced in Riverside. At one time, he was married, but this was while he was living in Tucson, Arizona. He came to Riverside just to have a change after the divorce was final.

It was during the fall of 1955 that Liz and Randy dated each other, quite often. Then, Randy asked Liz if she would like to bring Barbara and go to Catalina for a weekend visit.

They all went and it was so much fun for Barbara to take the ferry all the way there. Randy had an uncle who lived at Avalon Beach, and that is where they stayed and visited for the weekend.

At the dinner table one night, Barbara blurted out, "Randy, would you be my Daddy?"

"Barbara! Don't say things like that!"

Liz was so embarrassed. She had quite a long conversation with Barbara that night in private. She wanted to explain things to her so she would not make this mistake again.

Elizabeth and Randy continued to see each other. There was intimacy, but Liz made sure not to be anywhere near Barbara or home when this would occur.

It had been approximately six months and Randy was not interested in finally proposing even the idea of marriage. Although she liked Randy, and they seemed to have a lot in common with each other (except, of course, divorce), Elizabeth decided that it was time for some sort of seriousness to take place between her and Randy.

"Randy, do you love me, or is this just some sort of sexual fling that we are having?" Liz asked pointedly.

"I love you, Liz! I just don't want to get married. I really haven't gotten over my first marriage."

"Well, I can't go on like this. It isn't right, and I don't think I better see you anymore."

"Please, Liz! You've got to understand!"

"No! I must also consider my daughter."

So, they broke up. This hurt Elizabeth so much. She thought Randy was serious about her. Now, it was at least a relief to her that everything was final.

A Broken Heart

Oh, the ravage of a broken heart
Becomes an impediment to restart.

Lock my will not to hasten,
To follow sin for which I'm chastened.

Lord, my lonely heart cries to you,
Send me one who'll forever be true.

Senseless times have I experienced,
Only finding lust, the only preference.

Just a friend do I need,
Help me Lord to succeed.

A broken heart, it does heal,
But loneliness I always feel.

Help me Lord; I must endure,
Save my soul, and keep me pure.

John 15:15 ~ *Henceforth I call you not servants; for the servants knoweth not what his lord doeth: but I have called you friends; for all things that I have heard of my Father I have made known to you.*

Another Romance

Elizabeth decided that it would be better for her to take her daughter to a different church, to avoid seeing her former love, Randy. It was such a disappointment to have loved and lost. As it is said, "Life goes on."

Barbara was going on twelve years old, and spring of 1956 was passing fast, just as she wanted it to. She was looking forward to summer vacation from school. She had developed a number of good solid friendships, so she was happy. While daydreaming about summer, it so happened that the phone rang and Liz answered it.

"Elizabeth! Would you like to come to Malibu Beach and visit us this summer? You can bring Barbara and stay for a week."

"What a surprise! Yes, Vickie, we'd love to come. When should we come?"

"I'm not sure, but I wanted to ask you so you would keep it in mind. I'll call you a week ahead of time just to let you know."

Liz and Barbara went in the middle of June. Barbara had a wonderful time playing and swimming in the ocean with her two cousins.

After this little excursion, Barbara was a little sad to say good-bye to her cousins. They had had such a good time together. She was quickly reminded that she would see them during the holidays.

Through the years, after Edward died, Liz and her daughter became very close. They would talk about anything to each other, and, of course, swimming was the highlight of both of their lives. They were at the pool on the base one day, and while Barbara was swimming, a man came over to speak to Liz.

"I've been watching you while you were swimming. This must be one of your favorite sports. Is it?"

"Yes, my daughter and I love the water."

"I'm sorry. I should have introduced myself to you. My name is Dennis MacIntire, and I am currently serving my doctoral internship at Norco Naval Hospital. Being that you and your daughter swim so well, you might like to come to the pools at Norco Naval Base. One pool is Olympic sized for swimming and the other right next to it is for deep diving. It is up to twelve feet deep. Neither one is as crowded as this pool. Wouldn't you like to come sometime?"

"Well, I hardly know you."

"Don't worry. They are regular officer's pools, and I know you would be welcome to come over to Norco Naval Base."

"My name is Elizabeth Brennan. Thank you for the invitation."

"Do come next Saturday. I'll meet you there, and maybe we can get to know each other then. I must leave now. It's so nice to know you, but I have a meeting to go to."

Elizabeth thought to herself, "If he is an intern, he surely must be in his mid-twenties. He's much too young for me...but I would like to go swimming in that pool."

They went to Norco, and Liz got to know Dennis, who was twenty-eight. Even though Liz was eight years older than he, they dated each other for a few months. Then Liz realized, once again, that the relationship was not a good one.

Broken Hearts

Broken hearts, damaged in the throws of life
Reach to the Lord to somehow be revived.
Let us each day, pray to the Lord.
Broken hearts need assistance in this accord.

Live not each day for the world, it says in the Word.
Live with the joy of the Lord in your heart, in Him be
stirred.
Broken hearts are hard to mend.
That's why close to the Bible and praying you should
attend.

Be not weary or disappointed,
Just know you are with the Anointed.
He will comfort you in tribulation,
No matter your heartache or dissatisfaction.

A Focus On Transition

A thought ran into my mind about the woman alone, be she widowed or otherwise. There is a shocking transition which comes along with the fear of aloneness that captures her very thoughts and actions. At first, it hits with a feeling of a very large void inside of her. Later, the actual reality of her loss sets in.

There is a necessity to get things, as well as her thoughts, organized and to become grounded or secure in all of life's provisions. Sometimes, there is a defensive attitude that might develop. I guess this is a way of warding off the feeling of loneliness and helplessness.

We learn, when we are young, not to feel sorry for ourselves, but it is necessary to allot a time for mourning. If we don't do this, emotions will build up inside which can eventually overwhelm the mind.

Here is a picture of transition which I just happened to realize on one stormy day. I looked into the sky and saw many rolling storm clouds setting in the eastern part of the sky, but as I looked westward, the sky was a rich blue color, like a bright summer day. In time, the sun was blotted out, but through the clouds, it shone like a bright halo around the clouds. One would say that there's always a large brightness

at the end of every dark happening. You do have hope
in the Lord.

Our Great Savior

Jesus! What a Friend for sinners! Jesus! Lover of my soul; Friends may fail me, foes assail me, He, my Savior, makes me whole.

Chorus:
Hallelujah! What a Savior! Hallelujah! What a Friend! Saving, helping, keeping, loving, He is with me to the end.

Jesus! What a strength in weakness! Let me hide myself in Him; Tempted, tried, and sometimes failing, He, my strength, my vic'try wins.
Chorus

Jesus! What a help in sorrow! While the billows o'er me roll, Even when my heart is breaking, He, my comfort, helps my soul.
Chorus

Jesus! What a guide and keeper! While the tempest still is high, Storms about me, night o'ertakes me, He, my pilot, hears my cry.
Chorus

Jesus! I do now receive Him, More than all in Him I find, He hath granted me forgiveness, I am His and He is mine.
Chorus

Hymn written by J. Wilbur Chapman, composed by Rowland Princhard under the tune of *Hyfrydol*.

Symphony of Love

The Lord is the great maestro of all His creation,
We are like tiny notes and should flow in
synchronization.

 A great composition, a symphony of gold,
A rapture of completion will suddenly unfold.

Upon the return of Christ, so very suddenly,
He'll incinerate the notes of all uncertainty.

Right now, all the instruments are terribly off scale,
And many notes are missing because of one detail:

Many have wandered lost, and they have forgotten
It's for the Lord we live, for by Him we are begotten.

Mozart was an artist who was totally devoted
And for his love of music, it surely should be noted.

God's extended concerto will last forevermore.
And beyond the pearly gates, it will constantly soar.

Have you ever thought or had any conception
Of the total number of notes written for a complete
symphony?

Now, I'm not speaking of just one instrument,
And not the basic melody.

I'm speaking of the entire orchestration,
I'm talking in depth, you see.

The world is now composed of a musical menagerie,
Just pray and ask the Lord. He'll give you tranquility.

Though I cannot see Him, I know that He does live,
He'll answer all your prayers, on that I'm positive.

Your total love of the Lord erases all defeat,
Your acceptance of the Lord will make your life
complete.

The noble bells are ringing, the righteous harps
resound,
To make a joyous concert, so fine and so renowned.

Many centuries have passed since Christ died upon
the cross.
Soon, one day, He will come and punish all the lost.

Let not your heart grow cold, for otherwise you'll see
That you will be left out and will suffer hell for
eternity.

Lift your hearts right now before your death has occurred,
And later hear the symphony of love which, in this world, has never been heard.

May the Lord bless you and keep you.
He will, you can know.

John 14:10-17 ~ *"Believest thou not that I am in the Father, and the Father in me? The words that I speak unto you I speak not of myself: but the Father that dwelleth in me, he doeth the works. Believe me that I am in the Father, and the Father in me: or else believe me for the very works' sake. Verily, verily, I say unto you, He that believeth on me, the works that I do shall he do also; and greater works than these shall he do; because I go unto my Father. And whatsoever ye shall ask in my name, that will I do, that the Father may be glorified in the Son. If ye shall ask any thing in my name, I will do it. If ye love me, keep my commandments. And I will pray the Father, and he shall give you another Comforter, that he may abide with you for ever; Even the Spirit of truth; whom the world cannot receive, because it seeth him not, neither knoweth him: but ye know him; for he dwelleth with you, and shall be in you."*

1 John 5:10-13 ~ *He that believeth on the Son of God hath the witness in himself: he that believeth not God hath made him a liar; because he believeth not the record that God gave of his Son. And this is the record, that God hath given to us eternal life, and this life is in his Son. He that hath the Son hath life; and he that hath not the Son of God hath not life. These things have I written unto you that believe on the name of the Son of God; that ye may know that ye have eternal life, and that ye may believe on the name of the Son of God.*

Isaiah 19:20 ~ *And it shall be for a sign and for a witness unto the Lord of hosts in the land of Egypt: for they shall cry unto the Lord because of the oppressors, and he shall send them a savior, and a great one, and he shall deliver them.*

Isaiah 53:4-6 ~ *Surely He hath borne our griefs, and carried our sorrows: yet we did esteem him stricken, smitten of God, and afflicted. But he was wounded for our transgressions, he was bruised for our iniquities: the chastisement of our peace was upon him; and with his stripes we are healed. All we like sheep have gone astray; we have turned every one to his own way; and the Lord hath laid on him the iniquity of us all.*

Divorce - The Second Widowing

Having remarried in 1958, later in the year 1960 at the age of 40 years, my mother again suffered the loss of her second husband, this time due to a horrible divorce. However, she, being with the just born child of that husband, was given the strength to bring up that child alone, only with the help and encouragement of the Holy Spirit, who is also the comforter through all difficulties. Her faith was so rock hard strong that nothing could make her waiver or falter from her love for the Lord.

She knew that her only comforter and light in life was the Holy Spirit, who directs each person throughout his or her entire life if only he or she endeavors to ask the Lord into his or her heart and repents from sin and prays and follows the statutes and limitations of the Holy Bible, the Word of God.

No matter how many times one reads the Bible, there is always something new and important that pertains to his or her present being. There is always something new to learn.

Hebrews 4:12 says: *For the word of God is quick, and powerful, and sharper than any two-edged sword, piercing even to the dividing asunder of soul and spirit, and of joints and marrow, and is a discerner of the thoughts and intents of the heart.*

148

It is very important to remember that life on this earth can be likened to a small breeze, and that, while on this earth, it is all a learning process. If one keeps learning, along with studying the Bible, his or her life and faith will keep growing and strengthening. However, if one does not seek to follow the Lord's wishes, he or she merely stagnates to the point of nonexistence.

We are only in this world for a short time, to climb the mountain of life along the slippery rocks of trials and tribulations which are to teach us to hold fast to the all-powerful, gracious, and forgiving hand of God who has unlimited loving kindness for all of his children; even when the tidal waves of life can seem unbearable. These are a part of the molding and shaping of our lives into what can be a beautiful work of art which will be finally cleaned and polished for entrance into life ever after in heaven. This will be the time of graduation to peace and tranquility for evermore.

Matthew 5:16 says: *"Let your light so shine before men, that they may see your good works, and glorify your Father which is in heaven."*

Let not yourself fall by feeling sorry for yourself for the loss of your loved ones. Rather, think only of loving the Lord with all your heart, mind, soul and might. And be mindful of His work in you to help others to know the enrichment of His presence which is with you always.

Luke 10:27 says: ...*"Thou shalt love the Lord thy God with all thy heart, and with all thy soul, and with all thy strength, and with all thy mind; and thy neighbor as thyself."*

Ask and you shall receive, if you will just humble yourself to pray and believe that it also is "not my will, but Thy will be done," as the Lord Jesus prayed.

Luke 11:9 says: *"And I say unto you, Ask, and it shall be given you; seek, and ye shall find; knock, and it shall be opened unto you."*

It is commanded that we live for the Lord and not just our own selfish desires which, in the end, could confuse us about the true meaning of why we are alive in this earth.

Ephesians 4:22,23 says: *That ye put off concerning the former conversation the old man, which is corrupt according to the deceitful lusts; And be renewed in the spirit of your mind.*

May we always pray to the Lord in worship of the Holy Trinity and have thankfulness for the creation of God who wrote the most important book to learn and to follow: the Holy Bible. Be not afraid, for the Lord is with you always.

Psalms 23 says: *The Lord is my shepherd; I shall not want. He maketh me to lie down in green pastures: he leadeth me beside the still waters. He restoreth my soul: he leadeth me in the paths of righteousness for his name's sake. Yea, though I walk through the valley of the shadow of death, I will fear no evil: for thou art with me; thy rod and thy staff they comfort me. Thou preparest a table before me in the presence of mine enemies: thou anointest my head with oil; my cup runneth over. Surely goodness and mercy shall follow me all the days of my life: and I will dwell in the house of the Lord for ever.*

May your soul find the enrichment of the Father, the Son, and the Holy Spirit within you, too.

The Artist of Love

Supple my heart to be moulded and bent,
By Your loving hand which does not rent.

Just a tiny particle of dust am I,
To be included in Your work of art which you decry.

Let me not falter from your whole decree,
As the storm of night can break down a tree.

Impound in my heart neither to waiver
From the Spirit of Jesus, our holy Savior.

As I wake up to the new breaking of dawn,
Mould me and shape me to help others to live on.

Make me to be a part of Your grand orchestration,
Which forever will sound from your great revelation.

A tinker and a potter reveal their true source,
Thou gave us the Bible to direct our course.

If we become stubborn and uneasy to be bended,
You chastise our paths to soften us to be mended.

Help us, Oh Lord, to be fearful of your might,
So, in the end, we will shudder with joy upon Your
sight.

I have no fear of things happening in this world,
For you are the artist and in you we are pearled.

Not even a minute passes by that I sigh,
It's for You, Lord, I live; You are the Most High.

Temper my soul to follow You diligently,
Your Word and mandates to prosper and to be free

From all worries and sorrows which might hinder me,
And would keep me from the sight I now see.

Mold me and shape me to Your own special suit,
That I may help others and then produce fruit.

Not of my own doings, nor of my own works,
Rather Thy will is progressing and forever lurks.

The miracle of life which exists to this day,
How much more we should seek to repay,
By helping our kindred to finally find the right way.

We are like a team who should all work together,
Our direction of path should be towards life ever after,

With the Lord, the ultimate Artist.
Now, tell me just who could resist?

No, I really don't need to know of such fools,
Who refuse to accept and follow the golden rules.

May God richly bless you as He has me.

The Sickness and Death of Elizabeth

Elizabeth was all alone in Riverside, except for a few special occasions and holidays. She knew that she must keep herself busy, so she volunteered often at her church, and she joined Jack LaLanne's Health Spa to swim and get her exercise.

In May of 1980, Elizabeth felt a definite pain in her ribs and began coughing up blood. This scared her and so she went immediately to her doctor. Her first thought was that she might have tuberculosis; but then she thought it must not be. No one in her family had ever had it, and she wasn't ever, knowingly, exposed to it.

"Dr. Bingham, what is this that is causing me pain?" asked Liz.

"Elizabeth, I checked the tests, and you do have a case of tuberculosis. However, it is not transmittable for it is referred to as atypical tuberculosis. It can be cleared up, but that would require the removal of at least three of your ribs. I can't guarantee that the operation will successfully clear up the whole infection, but at this point, there is no choice but to operate."

"Well, when should I come for the operation?"

"The second week of June would be a good time. Actually, the sooner we operate, the more likely we'll be able to clear this up, before it spreads. Let

155

me confer with my colleagues and try to get the operation scheduled for a sooner date. I'll be in touch with you within the next few days."

In early June 1980, Dr. Bingham performed the operation. Sadly enough, it was learned later that not all the infection had been removed. The operation was not a success.

Even though she was in definite pain all the time, Liz still managed to take good care of herself and even go to the market. She was a well known customer and the people at her favorite store assisted her in every way they could.

Elizabeth lived for thirteen more years, during which time she would read the Bible daily and grew even closer to the Lord. She knew that the Lord was going to take her soon.

On September 19, 1993, Elizabeth died to this world and went to rest with the Lord. When the doctor pronounced her as dead, he looked at her face and saw a glimmer of a smile. His first reaction was to say, "She's a happy lady now."

Romans 8:17 ~ *And if children, then heirs; heirs of God, and joint-heirs with Christ; if so be that we suffer with him, that we may be also glorified together.*

The Storms of Life

When storms of life around you beat,
The way gets dark and drear,
With not one soul that you may greet,
Nor one to bring you cheer.

Your life seems very much alone,
You're passed on all four sides.
You wonder if still on the throne,
A loving God abides.

Though sick, sometimes nigh unto death,
You think your life is done.
Remember God, who holds the breath,
For you, and everyone.

Remember, too, that Job of old,
Lost sons and all his wealth,
And, in the Bible, we are told,
He also lost his health.

Yet, through it all, his faith in God,
These trials did not turn,
And when the testing fires were trod,
He did God's blessing earn.

So should your lot be hard to bear,
Your troubles never cease,
Just take them to the Lord in prayer
And he will give you peace.

And he, to the wind and wave,
Commanded: "Peace, be still!"
Stand with His arms outstretched to save,
And Keep you in His will.

Arthur J. Stairs

Psalms 107:28-30 ~ *Then they cry unto the Lord in their trouble, and he bringeth them out of their distresses. He maketh the storm a calm, so that the waves thereof are still. Then are they glad because they be quiet; so he bringeth them unto their desired haven.*

Strength Unveiled

Incandescent, can it be,
A life of perfect certainty.

Who can know, in reality,
What God intends for you and me?

When, by His light, I walk through darkness,
No fear have I, for He is sheer goodness.

So many children are born, upon the sunrise,
None of each knowing just what to surmise.

The Bible, the golden book of life, is all I need,
His Word is unsurmountable, full of trust and deed.

Hark, do I hear that much more must I learn,
To take heed and account for my personal discern?

It matters not from which waters we flow,
The endurance of faith in Jesus foils our foe.

The devil, with all unspeakable ways,
Tries to lure us like fish to go astray.

Though, at times, we find life hard to bear,
We should lean upon Jesus, for He does care.

Trials and tribulations are a big part of life,
To teach us all the lessons, some through strife.

Though we cry at the loss of those whom we love,
We should rejoice, for they've reached the kingdom
above.

Elizabeth lives on this day, as I read.
I'll think of her example and then take heed,

To go through life as a soldier, rearing my foe,
With Jesus as my armor, my suit, and my bow.

Elizabeth said, not alone am I, nor have I travailed.
Jesus and Jesus alone – my life's strength is unveiled.

9 780692 390276